No Rehearsal

D1563116

No Rehearsal

→→ A MEMOIR ←←

Brenda Bartella Peterson

GLOBAL MEMORY PRESS

ISBN: 978-0-9903450-0-8

LIBRARY OF CONGRESS CONTROL NUMBER: 2014909326

COVER PHOTO OF AUTHOR: JOHN LYNNER PETERSON
COVER ART & DESIGN: CAROL FOUNTAIN NIX
TEXT TYPESETTING & DESIGN: JONATHAN GREENE

Global Memory Press
P O Box 910265
Lexington, KY 40591

To John
you have plumbed the depths of my oceans
and transported me to the stars

To Tristan and Payden
you are my hope for the future

To Sims and Tiffiny
you have my eternal love

To Mark
you are my forever star
in the midnight sky

Contents

When one's young and doesn't feel a part of it yet,
the human condition; one does things because
they are not for good; everything is a rehearsal.
To be repeated ad lib, to be put right
when the curtain goes up in earnest.
One day you know that the curtain
was up all the time. That was
the performance.

—SYBILLE BEDFORD,
A Compass Error

Prologue
Before the Play Starts

Life can only be understood backwards,
but it must be lived forward.

— Søren Kierkegaard

"Mom," I asked, "Are we poor white trash or just poor?"

"Don't ask, honey, you don't want to know," she said, her voice tired.
I got my answer.

I attended 14 elementary schools. I never saw a Christmas tree two
years in a row in the same house until I turned 26 years old. My father
married nine times. My mother married four times. They married each
other three times. They couldn't make the relationship work, but they
couldn't stop loving each other. When I first put these facts together
years ago, I showed them to Mom. Annoyed I had put them on paper,
she replied in a flat tone, "Yeah, so what?"

I have married five times. My first husband died of complications of
multiple sclerosis from exposure to Agent Orange in Vietnam. My second
husband died of lung cancer. I married the third and fourth times as ill-
considered stabs at finding myself and my place in the world. My current
and last husband, my incarnate blessing, treasures the richness of our
life together as I do.

The impulse to write a memoir came from my desire to say that all
pain, sorrow, and suffering can be matched by joy, peace, and wholeness.
A life of challenge can still be a life worth living. On this journey I also
had to learn about forgiveness. Mark Twain said, "Forgiveness is the
fragrance that the violet sheds on the heel that has crushed it." Ah, the
irony that Violet was my mother's name.

Inability to forgive kept me from growing emotionally and spiritually since giving and receiving forgiveness are essential to moving forward. The biggest step lay in forgiving myself — a giant step in the direction of becoming real — a genuine person, not a role I crafted in response to what the people around me needed. I learned to forgive myself for not knowing the ordinary life skills that I had never been taught. I had to accept the fact the "you don't know that you don't know" when you are born in to poverty, chaos, and alcoholism. I had to forgive myself for having unreasonable expectations.

Life always, always has more to teach us. When I reached a role in life that I thought was safe, fulfilling and fun, tragedy had more to teach me about vulnerability. The secure, upper-middle class life I had created was not safe from the reality of death. So what role would I play next? Where is the route to wholeness now? The answers to these questions are part of what this book explores.

I wonder if the timid little girl, lips chapped red all the way up to her nose, mouth covered in fever blisters, would recognize the confident woman I have become. The waif who mothered all her siblings morphed into a brave, bossy, sassy survivor who can be herself. Who discovered that when she puts down her mask, she no longer feels isolated or responsible. If I could, I would reach back to tell that little girl the joy that comes when I'm just me. Writing this book is one way of doing that.

If a Japanese family owns an object of value, they treasure and care for it. But if the precious item gets broken, chipped or scarred, they brush off the damage with, "Now we can enjoy it." Using a technique called Kintsugi, families put gold in the broken seam of some items. I've learned to view my challenging life as an objet d'art with gold in some seams. Now I can enjoy it.

Act One

SCENE ONE

Memorializing My Raggedy- Ass Father

Many kids, it seemed, would find out that
their parents were flawed, messed-up people
later in life, and I didn't appreciate getting
to know it all so strong and early.

— AIMEE BENDER,
The Particular Sadness of Lemon Cake

Children begin by loving their parents;
as they grow older they judge them;
sometimes they forgive them.

— OSCAR WILDE

The call from my half-brother Dennis at 8:30 on a Monday morning could only mean one thing — Dad had died. The last few weeks, he had wandered in and out of consciousness, and we all knew he was ready to go. I have shed no tears since that day, but on the other hand, I have received a gift of healing I never thought possible as related to my Raggedy-Ass father.

Weeks before Dad's death, I had offered to do the funeral service. I knew officiating was a gift I could extend for my half-brothers that was unique to me. Then, leading the service was an abstract thought: One day I will preside over Dad's service. Now, reality hit me: In two days, in Evansville, Indiana, I will stand in front of others and say something about Dad. The downward spiral began with a conversation between my rational self and my irrational feelings.

What the hell was I thinking? I can't say something about him to even a small group of people.

I have to go through with it if for no one except Dennis and Greg. He was far more father to them than the rest of his scattered lot, but that's still a low bar to set for parenting.

I will not stand up there and say lies. I will not preside over a religious service for someone who, as far as I know, never entertained a spiritual thought in his life.

That narrowed down the repertoire for a funeral service drastically.

I sat in my comfortable chair all day Monday and read through three books of poetry hoping the light would dawn. No light dawned. I sent an email to Dennis, Greg and Margaret asking for memories of Dad. Surely, I will find material there. I asked my son Sims what came to mind when he thought of Pap-paw-on-the-river (my children's name for him). Their exposure to Dad was limited but Sims came up with the one word: fun.

As they had on so many occasions, my friends Don and Vonda Lichtenfelt brought wisdom and words. They arrived at our home on Tuesday morning with a file folder and books that might spark a flame and ease my anxiety. Those words from great thinkers sparked the magic, and by bedtime that night, I rested easy that I could speak to who he was and retain my sense of integrity.

Incongruous but true, Dad's favorite watering hole, Leroy's, owns a Facebook page. Their tribute stated he "sat at the corner bar stool, ordered a cheeseburger with onion and a 7 and 7. RIP Shoestring."

So I began the service at Alexander's Funeral Home West on Franklin Street in Evansville where Dad's father was eulogized in 1952 and his mother in 1992. I moved out from the lectern and pulled up a barstool. I invited everyone to join me in spirit at Leroy's, order their imaginary cheeseburger and maybe even a "smart alec" as we prepared to remember Shoestring. I made clear that we would honor Dad by keeping it real.

Kahlil Gibran wrote, "Life and death are one even as the river and sea are one." This rang true for the River Rat who spent many of his 87 years on the Ohio River and loved it as well as he loved any human.

No pretense or exaggeration was necessary to say we were remembering a unique and special character — truly one-of-kind. A River Rat, a brilliant contractor, builder, carpenter, bricklayer, a son, brother, husband (more than a few times), a father and friend.

Along with recounting the memories gleaned from my sibs, I also retold the story of his journey to the Super Inn in his wheelchair and how he got caught on the railroad track on the way home. My aunt, Aggie, Dad's only sibling present, shouted out from the audience, "It was probably a lie!"

Dad somehow missed out on winning a Pulitzer or a Nobel Peace Prize, an Oscar, Emmy or Tony award, but he did know the pleasure of small things:

> A full moon
> A four-pound bass
> A full hog on the spit
> A cold beer
> A fast boat
> A good day of skiing
> A good belly laugh
> And lots of women.

Dad built impressive structures all over the tri-state area with his hands and his intellect. He grew beautiful flowers in his back yard. He

roasted whole pigs in his BBQ pit and entertained the entire neighborhood. Although incapable of expressing it, Dad held the transcendent
in his heart, and that includes each of us.

There may have been a few among us that day who were old enough
to remember the play *Our Town* or maybe even played a part in that
classic while in high school. The character called the Stage Manager in
the play had this to say,

> Now, there are some things we all know, but we don't take
> 'em out and look at 'em very often. We all know that some-
> thing is eternal. And it ain't houses and it ain't names, and it
> ain't earth, and it ain't even the stars. Everybody knows in
> their bones that something is eternal, and that something
> has to do with human beings. All the greatest people ever
> lived have been telling us that for five thousand years, and
> yet you'd be surprised how people are always losing hold of
> it. There's something way down deep that's eternal about
> every human being.

That statement held true for Dad. His eternal something is us.
Through Dad's *numerous* branches on the family tree and our kids and
grandkids, Dad lives on. And I have seen in my own branch of this family tree that Dad's inheritance is a mighty strong one.

As I began to close the service, Aunt Aggie shouted out again. "You
know his name wasn't Clarence William Sims Sr. It was just Clarence
William Sims, no Senior."

It didn't seem *apropos* to argue with her that Dad became a senior
the minute they named my brother, Clarence William Sims Jr., so with
the mood of the last story destroyed I turned to what I know best and
closed with a prayer.

SCENE TWO

The Gypsy Years

If you have a skeleton in your closet,
take it out and dance with it.

— CAROLYN MACKENZIE

I became an adult the year I turned five. I knew it was time. Mom and
Dad splitting up — again — and Mom getting more and more off-kilter
came together in a way that told me someone has to be in charge of this
family.

That shotgun house on St. Joseph Avenue in Evansville was the only
place Dad lived with us. When he hooked up our first black-and-white
TV, our small living room lit up, and we were like a normal family, at
least "as seen on TV." Even as a kindergartener, I knew by some adult
measure that we were not like other families, but when we gathered
around that central glow, we faked normal in half-hour slices.

A few nights later, Dad came home late and drunk. Mom hit him
with the news that I had been chosen crown bearer on the queen's float
for the Festival Parade. All of Evansville waited on this festival every
year, and I needed a princess dress and a new pair of shoes. Dad wobbled
past her, heading for the bed without a word of response.

"Damn it, Clarence. Did you hear me?" her frustration held back
for hours already.

"I'm tahred. I'm goin' to bed," his only response.

She followed him carrying the only weapon close by: a big enamel
pan of dirty dishwater. I saw her anger rising, and the water flew toward

7

Dad, turning his dusty work clothes to mud. Dad's face sobered with shock and Mom's fury turned to fear. He swung his fist and the full force of his five-feet, eight-inch wiry body toward my terrified mother. She couldn't move fast enough and didn't match his strength.

In the house's single bedroom, between the kitchen and living room where that TV held my hopes of being a real family, I cowered in the corner as Mom screamed and dodged Dad's punches. I caught the combs that held back her thick chestnut hair as they flew in my direction when he whipped her around the room.

⋞ ⋞ ⋞

I remember as if viewing a grainy black-and-white TV image, I became an adult that kindergarten year, a role forced upon me but one I accepted as if it were my coronation. Getting the shoes and dress and riding on the float painted glitter over chaos. This episode was one of dozens of times Mom and Dad broke up and went back together — always a revolving door, never stopping long enough to provide something for me to lean on.

As I entered the world through elementary schools, the teachers did not seem to understand I was an adult and in charge of my family. Battle lines were drawn between me and teachers who wanted to control my mouth. When my second-grade teacher disciplined me for talking too much, she made me stay in the classroom alone while the rest of the class went to assembly. Then she turned the lights out. The room seemed scary and lonely, so I left and walked home. Staying there made no sense to me.

In fourth grade — the second time in my life I misbehaved — I received a U for "unsatisfactory conduct" on my report card — a dreadfully real scarlet letter for the little perfectionist. The teacher had warned the class that passing notes would result in a swift and universal red U. However,

9

I knew my friend needed my wisdom about the little boy she had a crush on, so I passed the note. Mortified when caught, I hung my head as the teacher meted out justice and sent us off to lunch. Brother Bill and I walked home for lunch as many children did (though no one was waiting at our house). Right away, I knew pride would not permit me to go back to school with a U on my report card. Bill returned after lunch. I did not.

After questioning Bill, my teacher sent him to retrieve the resolute and recalcitrant Brenda with a promise that the U would be painted over if I returned to school with a counter-promise never to pass another note. The message I took from this incident confirmed that I was, indeed, the one in charge.

During the nation's idyllic migration to the suburbs in the 1950s, my family moved from rented house to rented apartment to federal housing project. This nomadic lifestyle colored my childhood as sure as the western sunset colors the sky. The hottest summer in decades, 1953, we spent in a tiny upstairs apartment where a delivery man brought ice up in big blocks for the ice box. But my Least Favorite Award goes to another apartment — the one with an outhouse — yes, inside the city of Evansville during the Fifties. Could my lifelong intestinal issues have come from the terror of creepy-crawlies when perched over that rough-hewn wood? My tiny butt searched for balance over a hole big enough to swallow my body while my psyche fought fear. Looking back, I realize each dwelling place provided me with best and worst memories. The outhouse apartment came with a delightful old man next door who wanted to sharpen my *only* school pencil with his multi-purpose jackknife before the school year started. I, however, looked forward to using the school sharpener because I didn't want the task botched, but when he pushed, I could not say no. He carved a point so sharp and smooth, he used it as a cupid's arrow straight to my heart.

The best and worst of federal housing projects stun me when viewed through my rearview mirror. We lived in a black-and-white melting pot with pride. Our next-door African-American neighbors brought throw rugs and pillows over to make our apartment presentable when ex-in-laws visited. I remember dusty playgrounds with no grass and a wasp sting as the worst of the project, not racial tension. And, by the way, I liked the giant block of cheese every family got from welfare.

When I look at pictures of my childhood and reflect on them, I don't see "poor white trash" and didn't really feel like we were extremely poor. What I do see and remember is relentless instability, dysfunctional relationships and the constant moving about, always thinking life would be better "over there." Mom romanticized our rootless life: "I have a gypsy streak," she said and sang *Golden Earrings* in her smooth contralto voice. *"There is a story, the gypsies know is true — that when your love wears golden earrings, he'll return to you."* The connection of this romanticism to our vagabond life escaped me. My sister Margaret added to the embarrassment when she dubbed us "the new idiots," her own creative nomenclature because we were always the new kids in school. This condition was compounded by our being "the late idiots" because we couldn't get anywhere on time. My family dog-paddled for survival. Mom snickered and reminded us that Grandma and Grandpa Sims held the record for the fastest move because they decided to move to another house before they set up the bed rails in the current one.

As a child I had a recurring nightmare of living in a house on stilts being washed away by a mighty storm. I questioned the dream for years because we never lived on the ocean so why would I think my house would be on stilts and subject to storm waves? I then recalled that we did live in California for a very short time when I was a pre-schooler, long before the five years we spent there when I was in high school. An earthquake ate the Tehachpi Women's Prison during that same time. Reality, dream or metaphor, I knew home was fragile.

ᴒᴠᴒ ᴒᴠᴒ ᴒᴠᴒ

If I were to plan an imaginary dinner for my family at a local restaurant, we'd take the big round table in the corner. Older brother Bill, in bib overalls, no longer reeks of alcohol but his wrinkled skin, droopy eyelids, and dark circled eyes broadcasts that his body has not recovered even though his spirit is a perpetual "pink cloud." (Alcoholics Anonymous jargon for the euphoria from getting sober.) As he laughs too loudly and tells stories of drunken days and lost weekends, I see glimpses of the little boy and the teenager who greeted each day with "Hello world!" and wore a Japanese happy coat (generally translated to English as hapi or happi coat not happy) through much of high school. Bill could fix anything that needed fixing, especially diesel engines. During the worst of his drinking years, he worked for two companies that maintained big garbage trucks in the Chicago area. He would wear out the patience of one company with his priority on alcohol, and the other company would hire him by the next afternoon. One day on the job, Bill encountered something he could not control when one of the giant tires on a truck exploded at his chest. His injuries are not visible at this dinner, but they continued to scar his health the remainder of his life. Bill's logical explanation about The Incident that caused him to be a registered sex offender by the state of Florida hangs in the air at our light-hearted dinner. He was sober then, but perhaps his pink cloud drifted away on the day he raged at his mentally challenged stepdaughter and grabbed her breast. He explained that he was angry with her and her boyfriend for behavior inappropriate to her mental capacity. The judge didn't see it that way.

Pretending alone brings Bill to this dinner because his early life of drinking and smoking took the final toll, and Bill died of lung cancer at age 65 in 2010.

Sister Margaret arrives after Bill. Her outer appearance also reveals the choices she has made. Her anger worn thick like her mascara, her bitterness as brittle as the tenth coat of hot pink polish painted on her nails. I dig deep to find the bright little girl who skipped second grade or the quick sense of humor of her young adulthood. Margaret's laughter at a joke or situation that struck her as funny spread like news of the best shoe sale in town. Margaret blurts out as soon as she is seated, "Can you believe I have to have another surgery? This time for carpel tunnel syndrome." She delivers this news with excitement rather than resignation or frustration.

I wonder how someone as bright as Margaret cannot remember when to use she/her and he/him and they/them? When confronted or teased about her grammar, she tells you, rule by rule, the correct usage, yet refuses to use such rules in daily speech. This stubbornness completes the picture of refusing to get her undergraduate degree. For decades, she worked at a university where she could have finished for free. She dared to call colleagues "educated idiots" when they didn't see things her way.

Sister Ashley hobbles behind Margaret, the years of looking like Lynda Carter of "Wonder Woman" fame locked away in her memory. A run-in with a forklift on the factory floor interrupted her work life, sapped her will and drained her desires for years afterward. This waning of her will started early, but the accident squeezed its last breath. Her creativity, sensitivity, beauty, and wit might as well be specimens in the jars of a science lab for all the use they were to her. Ashley sparkled on stage when she sang and acted. Her sophomore year of high school, she stole the beauty pageant crown from all the seniors and walked away with the lead in the musical that same year. Her wit, even as a child, shined through in letters she wrote to me when I was in college. If Emerson is correct in saying, "What is needed in life is someone who will make us do what we are able," Ashley didn't have that someone in her life. I thought

I would be that person for her, then discovered I couldn't.

Our final sib, Vivian, may be the most fortunate in having less potential to work with. She wonders aloud, "Am I retarded?" We assure
her she's not, but comfort can't be found in some simple diagnosis. The
family shakes its corporate head and says, "She's just Vivian." Had she
been born a decade later, Vivian would have been diagnosed with multiple learning disorders. As a child, her waif look, quaint vocabulary and
general neediness manifested as Cosby-kid cute. Now that she's 40, these
characteristics evoke sadness and pity. Circumstances will require legal
intervention to protect one of her children from Vivian's lack of parenting skill. Her other child will spend time in prison — may still be there.
Vivian doesn't hobble physically as Ashley does, but the weight of her
mother-guilt rests so heavily on her psyche, no crutch or cane alleviates
the weight. Pretense also brings Viv to this dinner; she too succumbed
to an early death at age 47 in 2006.

At this imaginary dinner for which, I, of course, made the reserva-
tion — I order appetizers and resolve for the umpteenth time *not* to pick
up the whole check. I wear my excess of education like my expensive,
well-tailored Doncaster clothes. The skinny little girl whose crinoline
always hung below her skirt no longer exists. My smile, grooming and
practiced charm weave a curtain of denial that covers the pain, vulnerability and poor self-esteem of the Family Enabler Extraordinaire. And
at this point, I am still nurturing the notion I can redeem every embarrassing characteristic of my family with my own perfect behavior — an
exhausting not to mention arrogant, assumption on my part.

Then there's the general perception hanging in the air like humidity
in August that Brenda experiences no pain because "She has money and
a good man. My God, what more could she want?"

Oh, my, I sound bitter and angry. I must work on that.

As I pick my fingers raw (under the table, of course), my soul longs to be seen as a whole person by these people — fragile *and* strong and oh, so, imperfect. That's what I want. Perhaps an unreasonable request of people who are immersed in their own struggles and rendered myopic by their own pain. I bore the weight of guilt about rearing these siblings before I ever became a mother. My plan to use my college education to pull each of them along with me failed before I framed the diploma. This guilt rests like concrete blocks on both my shoulders.

Oh, I forgot, Mother is here.

Ashley surely chose Mother's too bright Wal-Mart dress, Margaret must have fixed her low-maintenance hairstyle and Vivi hovers over her expecting her to actually *be* a mother. Tall, big-boned, a bit overweight, Mother looks older than her years. Her high forehead and rectangular face hint at attractive but don't quite get there.

From her earliest encounters with motherhood, Violet Lee struggled. She laughs at herself and tells stories about her attempts at parenting like the day Bill swung a fish hook into my eyelid. She called a taxi to rush me to the hospital and left Bill, age six, alone on the sidewalk.

Surprise! Surprise! Dad arrives late. Perhaps we should honor him for showing up since he has built a life around the role of absent father. He doesn't have his pet pig in tow this evening and appears sober. At 86, he looks 105 and the self-proclaimed "shit-eatin'" grin that made all women between 12 and 60 weak-kneed now seems as rusted out as the moonshine still in his back yard. Dad pulled off this larger-than-life character with stunts. Friends flocked to his place on the Ohio River where an extra refrigerator devoid of shelves had its belly filled with a keg hooked up to an exterior spigot. Dad invented this decades before appliance companies got the idea to make water and ice accessible on the outside of the fridge door.

I cringe because I'm so afraid Dad will grab his chair, straddle it back-ward and order a "smart alec." I don't know what that drink is, but I

know he can't pull off the devil-may-care party animal anymore. At this pretend dinner, we laugh, have fun and never acknowledge or deal with realities like alcoholism, divorce, education, intimate relationships or caring for Mom or Dad when they're old. The strain put on the fabric of reality causes even the table, chairs and menus to tense the fibers of their being.

Relationships are essential to my very being. I need contact and interaction as everyone does but maybe more so because of the folks with whom I started life. For connection, I started with what I received biologically. Decades later, I continue to define relationships as the richness of life, and I am forced to admit, I started with *interesting* raw material.

ᘓᕲ ᘓᕲ ᘓᕲ

The Ohio River takes a horseshoe bend, so settlers came and the canal and railroad followed to create Evansville, my hometown. A massive influx of German immigrants around 1848, especially on the West Side where I spent some of my peripatetic childhood, gives Evansville a German flavor even today. During the Fifties the population hovered at 128,000, and folks still taught their children to play Clabber, a card game brought from Germany. Canal and railroad work turned into blue collar jobs through the decades. Sometimes Evansville was called River City, other times the Refrigerator Capital of the World because of Whirlpool. Evansville's major contribution to the nation came during World War II with a vast shipyard that built landing ship, tanks (LSTs). My mother worked there during the war, tightening screws that held together something, while my Dad served in the Navy. There was a college on the east side of town, but it seemed irrelevant to my family.

Clarence William Sims, Sr. stretched to call himself five feet eight inches. A Golden Gloves Bantam Weight boxing champion, Dad was wiry, athletic and smart — long torso, short legs and low-slung ass — I inherited all three. His white blond hair and crystal-clear blue eyes completed the image of *bon vivant*. He dropped out of high school and joined the Navy but was discharged after a diagnosis of rheumatic fever. With carpentry skills learned from his father, he expanded his knowledge to brick masonry and other construction expertise, enough to build whatever needed building. My Dad's hands built gorgeous limestone homes and tall office buildings in Evansville. With his intellect and expertise, he oversaw the building crews. The word-on-the-street indicated he could read a set of architectural plans and bid a job better than any contractor in town. Mom once pointed out to me that Dad and a man in our church whom I thought of as "rich folk" shared the same occupation. Sounds like Dad could have and should have had a successful career. To say Dad blew his career and a brilliant mind on wine, women and song would be a generous interpretation of Dad's career path — more like booze, broads and bawdy ballads.

I can't piece together the script of Dad's life chronologically. He came and went in my life. I longed for him in ways I couldn't name. Fragments of memory about him flickered behind a scrim and I couldn't blink away the haziness. I had to exert conscious effort to come up with clear episodes of interaction in the midst of the fog.

During my college years, I heard the phrase "lower class immediate gratification" in a psychology course. I knew the phrase applied to Dad. At times, he cashed his paycheck on Friday night, cavorted all weekend with the best of the rednecks and river rats at Dog Town (his little community along the river bottom on the outskirts of Evansville) and deposited what remained on Monday morning. When Dad graced the room along with the shit-kickin' country music, everybody partied. Even folks who didn't like him (probably for sound reasons) wouldn't deny they found him charming and engaging. Weekends on the river with the king of all River Rats and his speedboat enticed us all with the promise of fun and excitement. During my teen years, he let me drive the boat by myself. I beached the prized toy on a sand bar. Harsh reprimand about such an incident didn't fit his personality. He flashed That Grin and said, "Accidents happen when you're having fun."

I felt great sadness about Dad in his final years. He lived alone the last few decades, perhaps lonely, isolated on his glorious Ohio River. He grew up on the rolling waterway when his father ran a ferry boat taking people and cars between Indiana and Kentucky. At one point in his childhood, his family lived on a houseboat tied up on Pigeon Creek. He boated, skied and fished his river whenever time allowed and many times when it did not.

Any conversation requiring a degree of intimacy escaped Dad. Nine marriages indicated he was relationally handicapped, in spite of his considerable intellect. He didn't shrink from admitting he had tried nine times to be a husband. In fact, Dad displayed proudly a picture of himself and all six of his wives.

As you walked in the back door of his river house, the only door anyone ever used, the framed joke greeted you right there on the glassed-in porch. He must have been proud of it; he hung it up for all to see. Who put it together? Who found the pictures of all six wives? Chose the clever words? Knew that he married Mom three times and Lauren two? Probably some friend among his neighbors along The Bottom with whom he partied over the years.

The picture screamed of the reality that there is only one of him — in the center looking young, confident and vital — and six of them surrounding him. Us against him. Dad was a wall against which women threw themselves. Dad was good-looking, fun and, one would surmise, good in bed.

The words spoke as loudly as the pictures.

"The legend lives on."

"What every woman must know about."

"Getting around."

"I'm not her favorite anymore."

"Six Winning Teams."

"Exclusively you," appeared under the picture of Jerri, Dad's first wife. And "Nothing bashful about them, they're everywhere." Who knows what that meant?

Mom, either the biggest winner or the biggest loser because she married him the most times, sported the words, "Don't tell me, I know you want to ask me a question." Surely that referred to her need to communicate and his total inability to do so. And, by the way, I'm pissed that they used a middle-aged picture of Mom and young pictures of the other five wives. At one time, Mom was a beauty, too.

A gorgeous picture of Lauren came next. There were no bad pictures of her. Her caption read, "All's fair in love and war." That's an easy interpretation: Their love was more like war than love. She was supposed to be the classy goddess but she fought him like a man. Also beside her picture was the quote, "A small splurge now and then fills your jewel box with real gemstones. Smart girl!" No doubt Lauren extracted more from Dad materially than all his other wives together.

The picture for marriage six showed a seemingly innocent young girl. Betty was Dad's secretary and one of the affairs while married to Lauren. The word choice for her felt right, "Fantasy in a nice girl's life."

Then came the picture of Janet. There were no words that appeared to be connected with her. Perhaps her particular story with Dad loomed far too large for the artist to capture.

Finally, Irene was surrounded by the words, "One More Time" and "I'll take that challenge." That time the connection seemed to be alcohol. But she wasn't the last. Inexorably so, Dad remarried my Mom for the third time after his marriage to Irene. Then the fated divorce came, and Dad died alone and lonely.

I also have to admit when looking at this picture, that I, too, am one of the women who threw herself against that wall. I loved him and never felt loved by him.

ᘒ ᘒ ᘒ

Dad married Jerri Harrison, wife number one when she was 16 or 17 because she became pregnant with my half-sister Suzanne who grew-up to be a go-go dancer in downtown Evansville in the Sixties. That's the extent of what I know about her. Suzanne danced around the edges of my early childhood, but then I lost touch. Her stepfather adopted her and she didn't even share my name. When Dad lay dying in a nursing home in Evansville, a church choir came through singing to the patients. One woman from the choir leaned over his bed and asked, "Are you Clarence Sims?"

"Yeah."

"Do you know who I am?" she asked.

"Nah."

"I'm your oldest daughter."

When she walked into one end of the room at the funeral home visitation when Dad died, I nudged my half-brother Greg and asked, "Who's that? She looks just like me!"

"That's Suzanne, Dad's daughter by wife number one."

She is 70 now and a lovely person who reared five children on her own dancing and waiting tables.

ᘒ ᘒ ᘒ

My Mom, Violet Lee Marshall, wife number two, wife number three and wife number nine met Dad at Camp Reveal, a religious camp for underprivileged children when she was 12 and he was 14. Camp Reveal reappears a generation later when my brother and I will attend, which testifies to my parent's inability to escape the "underprivileged" moniker.

Mom loved Dad all of her life, hated him at times, but never got to the point of indifference — her goal at the end. I suppose he loved her, too. She often said, "He loves me in his way; he just don't weigh enough." She screamed at him, "You can think more and say less than any man on the planet."

Mother's engagement ring, a stunning, unique setting of rose gold with rubies and diamonds, carried part of their story. The ring constituted Mom and Dad's go-to credit source. They hocked the precious possession on numerous occasions. When Grandma rescued the ring, yet again, from the pawn shop, she announced to Mom, "You're not getting it back this time. Brenda gets it when she turns 16." So I did. Even *I* could not let go of the fantasy that Mom and Dad belonged together, so when they remarried the third time, I had the ring resized and gave it back to its original owner. Mom felt kind enough (or angry enough) to return it to me when the inevitable divorce came. The first divorce came shortly after my birth. That one occurred during the period when court proceedings were published in full transcript in the local newspaper. "Now comes the plaintiff with fuzz on the upper lip which appears to be a mustache" was printed for all to read. Even that embarrassment didn't preclude the inevitable; they remarried again soon. The first marital attempt produced my older brother Bill and me; sister Margaret came along during the second try. They divorced again when I was six.

చెం చెం చెం

Mom played card games at every opportunity. One night we chose Crazy Eights. Youngest sister Vivian was ten; I was 22 and married. Vivi, being young and more intellectually challenged than the rest of the family, was struggling with the game. Mom would not give an inch of allowance for Vivi. As Mom resisted cutting Vivi some slack, I teased, "God sure makes funny people mothers." We repeated the joke often through the years. We both knew the layers of meaning.

Mom grew to five feet eight inches by sixth grade, when teachers coerced her into playing the bass violin because she, alone, stood tall enough to hold the instrument. Her auburn hair, her best feature, caressed her shoulders in her younger years but later sported a frizzy perm. She laughed easily but stayed chronically depressed and chronically insecure. Her long fingers, her next best feature, pulled a cigarette from the package. Those hands could have been any movie star from the Forties, so graceful were her movements and so lovely were her nails. Then the tilt of her head and the thrust of her chin as the match and cigarette met drew the curtain down on any illusion of grace and sophistication. She shook the match until the flame died; she drew that first long breath with no fingers supporting the cigarette and squinted her eyes trying to avoid the ensuing smoke.

Mom never learned to pull off glamour or urban chic. The closest she came was the years she waitressed at the Vendome Hotel and strutted the downtown streets of Evansville in her Forties-style ankle-strap heels and her professionally coiffed chignon roll. I suspect she would have said I brought an end to that flicker of sophistication when her unexpected pregnancy with me occurred.

All mother/daughter relationships are complicated — ours proved uncommonly so. Perhaps we got off on the wrong foot because I turned one week old and she hadn't yet bothered to name me. Perhaps she'd already figured out motherhood wouldn't be her strong suit in life.

In spite of her parenting inadequacies, Mom's redeeming qualities shone through like shards of beach glass in the sand. She knew and lived out her belief that all human beings had value. As a child, I thought racism was a historical phenomenon no longer existing in the United States. I thought people like my Grandma Sims whose coarse comments about "niggers and Catholics" hailed from another time and place. Dad, with his backward and redneck ways, told my sister Margaret, "Your car looks like five families of niggers live in it." Irreparable. Disgusting. In Mom's world, racism didn't exist. We lived in federal housing projects during the Fifties where black neighbors played on the grassless playground with us and we never thought this unusual.

Multiple factors made motherhood a challenge for Violet Lee, but she would have made a fabulous librarian at her beloved Willard Library in Evansville. She required reading and books as much as the air she breathed. She once read all the books assigned to me in a college correspondence course. Then I sat with her and picked her brain to answer the questions in the written work. Her working-class family with an alcoholic father, growing up during The Great Depression and World War II precluded the possibility of college and a professional career. Her standard joke about her own siblings went like this, "My sister Juanita got all the talent; my sister Bertha Jane got all the brains, and I got all the kids." Though inaccurate, this perception added up to her lot in life. Her vocal talent alone could have led her in a different direction. During those waitressing years at the upscale Vendome, she had a fling with a guy who played in the band. They cut a record on which her beautiful contralto voice soared above his band. She also did not fall short on brains. She possessed a natural affinity for mathematics; consumed crossword puzzle books *using ink, not pencils;* and stored a vast array of history and trivia. My son Mark, whose intellect defined him, took several years during high school to reach his goal of beating Grandma in Trivial Pursuit.

Playing games must be listed among her strongest skills as mother. Mom taught us at very young ages to play all sorts of games, especially card games. We played one called *Authors* when Margaret was so young she couldn't say or remember Henry Wadsworth Longfellow, so we all identified him as Santa Claus so Margaret could play. Mom taught us to play Clabber as soon as we could grasp the concepts. Let's be generous and say, in her own way, Mom taught us logic, math and foresight — all required to play Clabber. Other skills, not related to games, were never taught. I inquired once as to why she didn't teach us to brush our teeth. She answered, "Buying the toothpaste and toothbrushes and putting them in the bathroom challenged me enough." Since Mom was defeated before the day began, having school supplies ready constituted a mountain she never once summitted. Not surprising, when my son started first grade, I obsessed for days over his lunch box, his pencils sharpened just right, his box of crayons the biggest available.

However, Mom taught us her favorite music, and singing together brings back my best memories of Mom. To this day, the music of the Forties tops my all-time favorites list. When other kids listened to the Big Bopper, Ricky Nelson and then the Beatles, I tuned in to Rosemary Clooney, Patti Paige, Frank Sinatra and the big bands of Glenn Miller and Tommy Dorsey. Sweet memories in a sea of turmoil. I sang every word of the Forties classics right along with her. Mom's fears and her children's often meant sleeping on pallets on the floor next to her bed rather than in bedrooms or beds. Floor-sleeping always included a radio tuned to the sounds of the Big Band Era that lulled us to sleep.

The *Reader's Digest Family Song Book* was tantamount to the Bible in our family. We often started the song on the next page without turning the pages or even looking at the book. With not a weak voice among Mother's five children, the best sounds came when we sang together in the car. Hymns, classics, nonsense songs, some country and, of course, the Forties popular music. At Mom's funeral, we sang *Back Home Again in Indiana — a capella*, like when we were kids.

Campell Soup kids with the Buster Brown haircuts, my brother Bill and I, two years apart, looked a great deal alike. Because I started first grade at five years old and "Bill got left in second grade," we journeyed through school one year apart. Why we called being held back a year "getting left" I don't know. He probably had ADHD (attention deficit-hyperactive disorder), but educators didn't diagnose or deal with ADHD yet. Close as children, we shared the Lincoln Library (a two-volume poor family's version of encyclopedias we owned with pride) when we did homework, and it wasn't unusual for me to do part of his homework. Wherever we went, we went together. Whatever we played, we played together. I knew every skinny joke because he used them on me. His favorite was, "If you stand sideways and stick out your tongue you will look like a zipper."

Mom assigned me the role of "designated achiever." I'm not sure why the mantle fell to me rather than Bill — probably because of his learning disabilities. In autograph books included with our school pictures one year, Mom sent clear messages regarding these assigned family roles. Bill was in fourth grade, and Mom wrote in his book: "As sure as the grass grows around the stump, you are my little Billy-Lump-Lump."

In my book she wrote: "Don't wait for your ship to come in, go out and meet it." I was just in third grade!

I felt hurt. Bill's message sounded gooey and loving. I didn't even understand mine. Mom tried to explain. She made matters worse. In my mind, her words to Bill showed love; what she wrote to me communicated expectation. Whether that was her intent or not, Bill and I lived out the truth of those messages in our futures.

By junior high, Bill created a scrapbook in which he recorded *my* achievements. He titled the book, "What Brenda's Done." Did Mom ask him to do the book? I don't know. We both played our assigned roles. I would like to think Bill enjoyed creative activities. We were close as children, and he inclined toward artistic tasks. So to lay out a scrapbook might have been fun for him.

SCENE THREE

Gumption & Grace

Here is your life. You might never have been,
but you are because the party wouldn't have been
complete without you. Here is the world. Beautiful and
terrible things will happen. Don't be afraid. I am with you.
Nothing can ever separate us. It's for you I created the universe.
I love you. There's only one catch. Like any other gift,
the gift of grace can be yours only if you'll reach out
and take it. There's nothing *you* have to do.
There's nothing you *have* to do.
There's nothing you have to *do.*
Maybe being able to reach out
and take it is a gift too.

— FREDERICK BUECHNER

My grandmothers dished up many meals during my Gypsy Years. In adulthood, I realized the kind of love my maternal grandmother gave us could be described as grace. If we wanted to, we could define grace as delight in another that comes unearned, undeserved and unexpected. Bertha Neuffer Marshall Whitmer, provided the grace note in my messy, abusive, neglectful childhood. In the too few years we shared, her smile broadcast the irrefutable truth: I deserved love. In adulthood, I discovered Frederick Buechner whose words concerning God's grace open this chapter. I knew at the bone marrow level this was the kind of grace I received from Grandma. Grandma personified God's grace.

Grandma's upbeat nature rarely wavered in spite of a life full of physically hard work, two alcoholic husbands and poverty. She cared little for outward appearance. She pulled her thin grey hair back in a rubber band. She could make her malleable face hilarious or scary and could produce wickedly funny sounds to entertain the nearest grand-child. No child's question met with an unwelcome response. I once asked for the recipe for mashed potatoes. Chuckling, she insisted "Mashed potatoes don't need a recipe!" But she showed me how to make them just right. No behavior ventured beyond her love. I once burned my midriff because I walked, with iron in hand, to eavesdrop on her phone conversation. My scar faded; the memory of her care did not.

Grandma taught us to recycle before recycling meant cool. The city garbage dump served as her favorite flea market and our Fifties version of Toys"R"Us. Grandma's enthusiasm prevented turning up my nose at the odor and any concern that shopping at the dump might not be quite right. Discoveries, often items I didn't know I needed or wanted, morphed into treasures seen through Grandma's eyes. Old purses, my personal fave; trinkets for house or garden appealed to Grandma, and a special rock to place around the fish pond delighted all of us — no found object lacked possibility.

Many springs, Grandma escorted me around her yard on North Kentucky Avenue in Evansville as she recited the names of every flower in bloom. While not excited about horticulture lessons, my gut told me time with Grandma cultivated within me the feeling of being loved un-conditionally that I craved. Even now I experience lingering grace notes when flower names pop into my mind from some ancient, cobwebby index. Pansies, creeping phlox, hydrangeas, geraniums. I walk down any street, identify each plant and my heart blooms with memories.

In contrast, a day in the blackberry patch with Grandma pushed me to the edge of my comfort zone. I don't like to sweat. I don't like being stabbed by brambles. I don't like chigger bites. With a bucket full of blackberries and enough sassafras to boil for tea, we wandered back to Grandma's house. As I rubbed her gnarly feet after the almost-worth-it cobbler and tea, a tick sauntered down her forehead. I screamed. Grandma removed the tick with a surgeon's care and instructed me that we must burn ticks instead of squashing them. Grandma's exposition on the death of the tick commanded equal time to her explanation of the benefits of sassafras to the next generation — neither got rushed. As I moisturized those old diabetic feet, the minutes were filled with stories and wisdom — and grace.

Sometimes grace needed dispensation in the middle of the night. If Mom got scared for no earthly reason, or some reason she refused to reveal to the kids, she loaded us up and off we went to Grandma's — in a taxi. *Normal* families in our town didn't use taxis during the day, much less in the middle of the night. Dressed in her ragged chenille bathrobe, Grandma greeted us and paid the taxi fare, and we felt secure. We were ushered to pallets on the floor; Mom received comfort about her fear *du jour*.

Grandma's dispensation of unconditional love shone in high relief against my self-doubt, instability and turmoil. While I found other sources of support outside the family, Grandma's bottomless well of affirmation inside my family gave me the message I was a person of value. I deserved love, time and attention. Psychologists now confirm that children from poor and/or dysfunctional homes can survive and thrive if a message of worth comes from a single source — a compassionate witness to their lives — someone to hold up the mirror and reveal they are a person of value. Those researchers must have studied my grandma.

∾ ∾ ∾

If nothing is going well, call your grandmother.

ITALIAN PROVERB

Grandma Sims, my dad's mother, provided a study in contrast to my grace-filled Grandma. If the word fun and Grandma Sims were used in the same sentence, I never heard it. She embodied all business, all the time — grit and gumption. She cooked, cleaned, sewed and brought order to disorder around the clock. I don't remember her sitting down. I loved the sense of organization pervading Grandma's house.

Grandma expressed love for me through these same skills. Her face lit up when she saw me and she gave warm hugs; beyond that, she expressed her love with action. She washed, ironed and mended with the expertise of the finest tailors whatever clothes I had with me when I stayed at her house. Fresh bread, lunch meat and homegrown tomatoes, standard in her immaculate refrigerator, made sandwiches at Grandma's taste like gourmet fare. The *piece de resistance*: Grandma's homemade biscuits dipped in a swirled-together mess of white Karo syrup and peanut butter. This may not top your list of big deals, but my house did not come with full, clean refrigerators and homemade treats.

Grandma had eight children and an alcoholic husband. Hard work was her norm. Big gatherings at her house were raucous occasions smoothed over with delicious food. The family lore asserted you could count on someone "to show their ass" at every Christmas gathering. (Do I need to explain here that we didn't use the phrase literally?) One Christmas, the bare ass belonged to Grandma — if you can call getting angry with Grandpa and throwing a fit The Traditional Showing of Ass. Grandpa Sims, an expert carpenter, built me an exquisite wooden kitchen — every little girl's dream. Grandma pitched a giant fit because he hadn't made one for their other granddaughter. I suspect Grandpa's neglect was due to a shortage of time rather than affection, but Grandma's tantrum expressed her displeasure.

Grandma spewed bigoted and opinionated views freely. She used the terms "niggers and Catholics" in pejorative tones leaving no doubt about her judgment of entire groups of people about whom she had little knowledge. She didn't graduate from high school, and if she desired to learn and inform herself outside of school, I never heard her talk about it.

Grandma fought crippling osteoarthritis, and doctors told her to never stop moving her hands lest they draw up in knots. She moved to a nursing home in her 80s diagnosed with Alzheimer's. She assumed they needed her there to run the place. My sons guffawed when they heard this story about Grandma and said, "That's exactly the way you will be, Mom. You'll think you're in charge 'til the day you die." No question, much my heritage for persistence and bossiness came from Grandma Sims.

Grandma Sims' action-oriented love showed me a very different form of love than my grace-filled grandma's, but I got the message: She loved me. From an adult retrospective, I wonder what Grandma would have done had I possessed the courage to tell her my aunt/her daughter molested me when I was five and living with the two of them.

SCENE FOUR

Namesake & Blueprint

Without heroes, we are all plain people,
and don't know how far we can go.

— BERNARD MALAMUD

I was eight days old and Mom still had not named me. Mother's younger sister Bertha Jane, 16 at the time, came into the hospital with a plan. So shy she couldn't lift her head to talk to her own sister, she stared at her feet and asked, "Could I please name her?"

Thus, I became Brenda Jane. The Jane portion carried a long history from aunt to niece in our family and came with a spectacular hand-cut diamond cluster ring that had originated with my Great-Aunt Jane, who worked for her sister, a professional madam. The Brenda portion came from Aunt BJ's pen pal in England. Always grateful I escaped the Bertha part of her name, I learned years later she also hated "Bertha." So after the original Bertha's death (my grandma/her mother), she changed Bertha Jane to BJ.

This act of naming created a tether reaching across continents in our later lives. Aunt BJ lived elsewhere much of my childhood — away at college, graduate school, seminary and then twenty years as a Baptist missionary — but she provided the only model on Mother's side of the family for how to pursue a college education. I claimed this inspiration for better or worse. When she came home for visits, I knew she represented a world beyond what I experienced with my mom and stepdad, and I wanted to know such a world. While on furlough from Japan, Aunt BJ stopped to visit us in California. Two memories left etchings in my brain from that visit. She had a suitcase full of Japanese silk for souvenirs and to exhibit at the many

speeches she would give. As Aunt BJ searched through the suitcase for something, she screamed as though frightened. A big black crusty cockroach dared to cross the boundary between our pitiful existence and Aunt BJ's world-beyond-our-family, that Maginot Line between my family of origin and the future I saw for myself. On the same visit she declared, "I don't know why I go halfway around the world to teach the English language when my own family doesn't speak it." These memories were etched with a quill of shame.

SCENE FIVE

A Child in Charge

Just as we develop our physical muscles
through overcoming opposition — such as
lifting weights — we develop our character muscles
by overcoming challenges and adversity

— STEPHEN COVEY

On a sweltering July day in 1954, the children of welfare families in Evansville were loaded on to buses and taken to Yabrody Park. This venue, a pitiful excuse for an amusement park, might well have been Disney World for us. My brother Bill was nine; I was seven. Before we got off the bus, the supervisors told us everything in the park was free today. We could ride the rides as often as we liked, play the games; anything we wanted to do.

Bill and I darted off to have some fun. We delighted in every sight and sound, escaped our everyday realities and soon got thirsty. We walked to the little wooden shack concession stand and Bill ordered two Cokes. The lady handed them to us; I took a sip of mine and then she said, "That's fifty cents." Bill and I looked at each other dismayed. He found his voice first and said, "We don't have any money. We were told everything in the park is free for us today." The lady glared at us with disgust and said, "Go ahead and keep them. Your sister already drunk out of hers. You welfare kids are all alike. You think everything ought to be given to you!" The shame, humiliation and degradation I felt wounded me so deeply; it left emotional residue that remains today

39

though I am an accomplished, financially secure adult. That sense of shame pervaded my childhood.

That same year the telephone company in Evansville chose my family as their annual welfare family to give Christmas presents to. My sibs and I were asked to make a list for Santa Claus. Every little girl in my class wanted a bride doll that year so in my best third-grade printing I wrote "bride doll" at the top of my list. My excitement on Christmas morning made my tummy flip-flop. Many more presents than usual crowded our tiny living room at the Sweetser Housing Project. Finally, my turn came to open the biggest box from Santa. Excitement didn't allow time to be careful with the paper so I ripped and tore until the doll inside revealed herself to me. An obviously used doll in a pitiful excuse for a white satin dress lay limp in the box. My first thought was not "it's the thought that counts and the phone employees were doing something nice." My heart wanted to know, "Why doesn't Santa love me enough to give me the kind of bride doll all the other girls are getting?" My lack of affection for the doll showed up a few months later, when Mom asked, "Where is the doll you got for Christmas?" With nonchalance, I replied, "Oh you mean the one Billy hit in the head with an ax?" My brother used the pitiful bride to practice killing people.

⤕ ⤕ ⤕

Religious experience started for me at Camp Reveal. Pappy Reveal, a non-denominational evangelical minister, founded The Rescue Mission for the drunk and homeless in downtown Evansville and Camp Reveal on the outskirts of town for underprivileged children. If Pappy had a first name other than Pappy, no one knew. Mom and Dad attended this camp as children, so my brother Bill and I went also. I suppose a free camp gave Mom a respite from the two of us and met her criteria for a good camp. I remember excitement about going and, at first, no knowledge the camp was for poor kids. I knew the family lore that Mom and Dad had met there.

During my summer there as a five year old, I sang in public for the first time at Wednesday night camp fire. My aunt prepped me and I performed *Don't Do a Half Day's Work for the Lord and Expect a Whole Day's Pay*. Today I can't sing the song without sarcasm, then I sounded like a sincere little angel-choir-of-one.

> *Don't do a half day's work for the Lord and expect a whole day's pay.*
> *Only what's done with all of your heart, counts on the judgment day.*
> *How can you stand idly by, knowing souls are doomed to die?*
> *Don't do a half day's work for the Lord and expect a whole day's pay.*

I won third place or, maybe, first. Now I question the theology of the chorus. At the time, I didn't comprehend what a heavy spiritual load the song laid on a five year old. I dodged the guilt, at least for a few more years, because in my little girl mind winning the contest took precedence over pleasing the Lord.

At age nine, I 'got saved' at Camp Reveal. At a late night service in the big building when tears and remorse flowed freely, I walked down the aisle and confessed my nine year old sins. I probably waited until the tenth time we sang *Softly and Tenderly*. In retrospect, no wonder I responded to the mournful crooning of *Come home. Come ho–oo–ome. Ye who are weary, come ho–oo–ome*. Since "home" changed so frequently, I couldn't identify the word with a place, I must have been drawn to the notion I could find home somewhere, somehow.

On Friday nights at Camp Reveal, we hiked to the foot of the cross which marked the entrance of the camp. When a car passed on the country road, the campers called out "graveyard" in a sing-song manner which supposedly encouraged little hikers to get off the road so we didn't end up in the graveyard. My short legs remember the hike as 20 miles long, reality insists more like two. The cross signaled the existence of the camp for passersby on old Highway 41 in Evansville. My childhood perceptions again exaggerated size. The cross stood 50 feet tall in my memory; later years confirmed it was more like eight. Made of wood and wired for electric lighting, the image proclaimed brightly for the entire sinful world to see that "Jesus Saves" in neon letters. We sat at the foot of the cross on those hot summer nights and sang *The Old Rugged Cross*, gave testimonies and wallowed in the culpability of our wayward existence. Even at age nine, I knew I was a sinner saved by grace and Pappy Reveal. Pappy, a charismatic stump of a man, got whole cows donated to his ministry of saving the wretched children of the poor.

Grace Baptist Church in Evansville reinforced the theology I learned at Camp Reveal. Though my family moved *all* over town, this church provided some consistency in my unruly childhood. Decades later I realized the radical fundamentalism of their theology. Various family members belonged to this church but most significantly, Aunt BJ. God and this congregation led her to become a missionary. Her picture still hangs in the church.

My best friends at Grace Baptist were Christa and Becky Woods. On many occasions, we walked the one block to Francis Pharmacy after church where we sat in a booth and shared a Coke and plate of French fries. When the fries were gone, we put salt and ketchup in the grease and licked up yummy flavor with our fingers to stretch the taste a few more bites. We no doubt were waiting on Mazo and Tom Woods, their parents, to finish some meeting so we could go on home. Many nights at the Woods' home, I glimpsed what *real* families lived like. They gathered around their parents' bed, read scripture and prayed before going to bed. Mesmerized by those kinds of moments together, I thought their house and family idyllic — a white-picket-fence-type existence. Mazo, the organist at the church, rehearsed with me at their home on the little spinet piano, and I sang in church long before I could see over the pulpit. I practiced "Longing for Jesus" with her until Christa and Becky started spoofing the song in the other room. Music *and* friends *and* doting parents *and* a lovely, organized home — I had died and gone to heaven.

I won the Sword Drill championship at Grace Baptist Church. The militaristic Bible Sword Drill required memorization of many Bible verses but also the training and skill to find those verses in the Bible. Children stood in a line like young warriors for the Lord.

"Attention!" the instructor called as we stood military straight with our regulation Bibles at our sides.

"Draw swords!" Bibles raised to waist height with one hand on the bottom and one hand on the top, *no* fingers curled over the sides.

"John 3:16. Charge!"

At the command, we turned pages until we placed a finger on the right verse, looked up at the judges and *then* stepped forward. I carried monster guilt for years because I once stepped forward and realized — even though the judge did not call on me to read — my finger rested on the wrong verse. Rules demanded you rat yourself out if that happened. I realized my error as we stepped back for the next round — despite shame and guilt, I never told a soul. Until now.

Having won the local contest, I was eligible to participate at the state level in Indianapolis. A young couple from Grace Baptist agreed to give me a ride to the convention, and I would stay in Christa and Becky's hotel room with them. As usual, my stomach knotted up with excitement and anticipation. I felt important, adventurous and worldly heading out to a big city with the determination to win it all and impress every one at home.

The miles in the back seat with my sensitive tummy resulted in motion sickness layered over excitement. I fought the urge as long as I could, but the wicked vomit spewed just before we hit Indianapolis. How was

I supposed to tell these strangers I had to throwup? My dress and shoes now reeked of bile, and the spotless car of the sweet young couple smelled strongly of my wretched lack of sophistication. I felt my white trash status cut through my thin layer of nail polish lacquered on for my big trip.

That young couple treated me with care and compassion, it was my internal dialogue that criticized me for not knowing how to communicate and function in the larger world. I allowed a small malady like motion sickness to become a judgment on my character.

ക്ക ക്ക ക്ക

When I was nine year old, my five-year-old sister Margaret was diagnosed with cirrhosis of the liver, *and* new baby sister Ashley developed spinal meningitis. The whole family grew tense and scared as my little sisters lay in two hospital rooms down the hall from each other. This was serious stuff. I threw a whopper tantrum so Mom would get the pastor to come over to the hospital. You see, I knew, at ten years old, my little sisters had to "get saved" to ensure they did not burn in hell if they died.

What kind of church teaches children that other children will go to hell? Nothing I learned in churches for many years disabused me of this notion.

Decades later, a friend in Kentucky told me he once interviewed to pastor Grace Baptist Church in Evansville. He turned them down saying, "I can't be pastor of a church which professes only what we *shouldn't* do as Christians instead of what we actually do." Gratitude cascades over me for adults in those Baptist churches who nurtured me, but I also experienced the shallow, prejudiced, narrow beliefs as another violation of trust — a spiritual abuse.

ക്ക ക്ക ക്ക

Mom's struggle with parenthood intensified between her marriages. My fourth-grade year, one of the worst periods, we went to five different schools. Her work outside the home along with motherhood overwhelmed her before the day got started. One house and one job created a situation wherein she left for work 15 to 30 minutes before we left for school. We jumped from the top bunk onto Mom's full-size bed in the same small room to entertain ourselves in the short span between her departure and ours. Clueless of the damage possible to children and mattress, we had fun. When Mom found out about our shenanigans before school, she hired a friend of Grandma's who seemed to be 101 years old. She wore torn up rags in her panties due to incontinence. She rinsed the rags and hung them around the bathroom — gross! But her fried apple pies made up for this shortcoming. And, of course, we knew she wouldn't last long because nothing did.

One weekend morning during this period, Mom announced, "I've got a secret. Your hint is the box of oatmeal." Disgusted with my inability to guess the secret, she explained, "The oatmeal brand name — Wedding Oats! I'm getting married."

We had met this guy Elvie and he did not impress me. Lack of knowledge held me back not a whit from this opinion. At nine, I assumed a great deal of authority over Mom, little sister and big brother. I knew I needed to care for them. I knew I could be boss. I asked myself, "*Would this mean one more person I have to be in charge of?*" At nine, my authority was more emotional than practical. My disapproval or temper tantrum would let Mom know I thought she needed to make a different decision. Later my control developed practical applications: caring for my siblings, cooking, cleaning, running the house. For better or worse, my disapproval and accompanying tantrum waylaid Elvie and the marriage — too much power and authority for one so young.

I realize now that I assumed the role of parent so Mom could still be a child, a charming child at times. We laughed a lot. Played games. Sang songs. But I knew and she knew I held the power. I didn't require discipline at home, so I slipped into the role of adult with ease.

Dad made rare appearances during those years. He was the character actor who added so much to the story in spite of being on stage just a few minutes. Behind the scrim through which I saw him, I remember how he found babies and small children irresistible. During the short period he lived with us on St. Joseph Avenue, he and his buddy Shorty Neece took care of us kids one night while the moms went out. To occupy Shorty's wild-child three-year-old, Dad put molasses on the boy's fingers and gave him a feather.

"Now, give that feather back to me, boy."

Dad and Shorty laughed and teased and enjoyed the joke. Dad stayed "at the ready" for fun. As he played with one of the babies, I remember him saying, "You ain't good for nuthin' but it sure is fun whittlin' you out."

❧ ❧ ❧

Mom married Herman Lee Bennett that same year she dated Elvie. She became pregnant with my half-sister Ashley, thus speeding up the wedding plans. This marriage added a modicum of security to our lives because of Herman's steady job. In the beginning, I felt proud. The addition of handsome, big-muscled Herman meant we no longer bore the atypical (for the Fifties) moniker of single-mom-divorced family. My authoritarian role in the family hit a bump with this marriage because Herman didn't take well to a nine-year-old being in charge. He seemed shocked as that first year progressed and I diapered, dressed and cared for Ashley as well as Margaret and without doubt bossed Bill around, too. While Herman's objection did little to change the way Mom and I related to each other, he took some of my power with the sheer force of his physical presence in the family.

The steady job didn't change everything. Life still happens. One day when I came home from school for lunch, Mother sat at the Formica table, a can of peas, buttered bread and coffee for her lunch. I hated that house close to Delaware School and particularly the kitchen. Herman painted the linoleum with a bizarre abstract pattern to cover his bad base coat. When you turned on the light in the dark of night, those giant, crusty-backed cockroaches scrambled for cover — *hundreds* of them. To my nine-year-old mind, the roaches, the bizarrely painted linoleum, a mother who ate only peas for lunch and the shame of our poverty-stricken dysfunctional family connected in ways as strange as the linoleum pattern. Surely, if Mom could pull off the June Cleaver act with diagonally cut lunch meat sandwiches and freshly coiffed hair, our lives would improve. But she sat around in her red chenille bathrobe, smoked cigarettes and worked crossword puzzles and looked more like a hung-over Cher than June or Donna Reed — and she didn't even drink.

Mom tried — she really did — on some days. She tried to make sure I had a new dress around Christmas and my birthday because she knew the church would be toting me here and there to sing for adult Christmas functions. That year my dress, a very muted dull pink corduroy seemed to make my annual mouth full of fever blisters shine brighter than the dress. I pretended to like the dress because Mom tried.

Only adulthood allowed me to realize how depressed Mom must have been for much of my childhood. I just wanted her to figure out what was causing the additional children so they would stop coming. During the period of bad linoleum and cockroaches, she had more reason to be stressed and worried. It was the same time as Margaret's and Ashley's critical illnesses. I had held Margaret and changed her diaper before I even started first grade. I learned early on she was a strong-willed child who banged her head on the wall and her crib until her forehead was bruised. With no known cure or even much knowledge of cirrhosis of the liver in children, the doctors pumped her full of steroids in an attempt to save her life. Her cute little chubby cheeked face looked like someone put a straw in her ear and blew her up when side effects of the steroids reached their peak. Her body recovered from the cirrhosis, but the steroids left some permanent damage.

The doctor appointments, medical procedures, hospital stays, injections, scars and medical personnel from that period schooled Margaret in the role of a sick person. She learned her lessons well and never developed an identity as a well person.

Margaret would continue to look up to me as mother, sister, fixer, bank and friend. Until she thought I was no longer able to rescue her or was no longer willing.

With a full head of dark hair and deep blue eyes surrounded by black lashes, little Ashley was the most beautiful baby I had ever seen. Of course, I cared for her from the beginning. She lay in a bassinet beside Mom and Herman's bed. With respiratory problems from the start, she kicked one of her tiny legs up high enough to touch the scalding hot snout of the vaporizer and burned herself so deeply it scarred her leg. Sometimes Mom even awakened me during the night to care for her when she was a newborn. In fifth grade at the time, I resisted getting up.

"Mom, I'm too sleepy. You know I don't do well when I lose sleep."

"Go on back to bed," she grumped back at me. "But you are not allowed to touch her again. Ever!"

She never held to such threats, and that one was over by time I got home from school the next day. But she pouted for days. I knew the role required of me, and Mom's pouting was fierce motivation for me to learn my part well. I hated disappointing her. I was supposed to take care of her so well, she would never be unhappy with me. At least one other time when I complained about caring for Ashley in the middle of the night, Mom got furious with me. Maybe a clean diaper will make her feel better, I thought. So I diapered the baby and handed her back to Mom. She just returned Ashley to me and put her head down on the table and sobbed.

Herman couldn't handle the stress of two sick kids so he made an exit. I awakened one night during this period to discover my Dad on the couch with Mom. Once again, he entered for a quick appearance. I tried to figure out if the stress was too much for Dad as well because he didn't stay and Herman returned. My nine-year-old mind tried to make sense of Mom and Dad on the couch that night — I couldn't figure out what to make of their being together, if anything. Dad was soon gone again so I filed it under — another brief encounter.

From the crazy-painted kitchen, Mom's voice drifted toward me. She and Herman were fighting — again.

"I'd say you don't have the right to know why I had my ex over that night. You walked out on me when I had two children in the hospital — not knowing whether either of them would live!"

"I couldn't stand one more ounce of pressure from this damn bunch! I work hard all day, and all I get at night is crying kids and exhausted wife," Herman yelled back.

"Well, aren't you pitiful. How do you think the kids and I feel? This is serious shit. Ashley and Margaret are sick!"

"I know. I know," Herman screamed back, louder with each sentence. "I just didn't think it would be like this."

"Well, I guess we should have thought about that before I got pregnant when we were dating. It's a little late now."

With time, Margaret and Ashley recovered from their illnesses. We moved on to more houses. Mom and Herman muddled along in the marriage.

చిశ చిశ చిశ

The year I turned 12, Dad asked if I could come live with him and gorgeous young stepmom Lauren, so I could help care for their four-year-old child — my half-brother William Dennis Sims.

Lauren, a high school senior, was the affair Dad had during his second marriage to Mom. Lauren became pregnant while still in high school so he divorced Mom and married her. She and Dad broke up and got back together more times than Liz Taylor and Richard Burton but married only twice, making her wife number four and five. A second half-brother, Gregory Lee Sims, came along during the back-and-forth dance. Mom said Lauren succeeded a bit more with Dad because she fought him like a man. Family lore holds she once almost killed him when she struck him over the head with a telephone — remember telephones were once heavy. It was hard to imagine the woman he called his "classy pussy" fought him physically, but the stories made good family gossip and have since been confirmed by her son. Whether or not her success derived from the physical fights, she exhibited more ability to bend him to her ways than the other wives did. The homes he shared with Lauren, the amount of child support he paid to the children he fathered with her, and maybe a dent in his manners and dress, testified to her greater influence over him. Although I did witness him at dinner with her, his customary foot on the chair, knee up and one arm around that knee as he ate. No one tamed the beast.

Excited to live in a more organized home with only one sibling, I jumped at the chance to move in. The little house at 307 Enlow Avenue in Evansville thrilled me with its middle-class look, cleanliness and organization. Lauren loved clothes as much as I did and provided me with new outfits and new perspectives — even if she did insult my 12-year-old womanhood by saying my bra cups were about the size of 50 cent pieces.

She challenged my religious beliefs by asking, "Do you really believe all that stuff you're memorizing for the church?" — the first and only person in my childhood who expected me to defend what I believed. She put her high school typing book beside the typewriter and challenged me to teach myself to type. As I sit here typing this manuscript, I'm grateful for this skill, which has served me continuously since sixth grade.

The day after Christmas, we heard a knock on the door. Lauren, little Denny and I all ran to the door. Dad was at work. The stranger at the door said, "M'am, I think you should know your husband is having an affair with my wife."

All hell broke loose. Lauren tossed Dad and me out as soon as he got home. He dumped me at the tiny apartment where my Mom, stepdad and three other siblings lived. Gorgeous young stepmom took all my Christmas presents — including a fabulous little baby-blue-and-brown dress made of polished cotton — back to the stores. She discovered Dad used me to baby-sit Dennis while he met the other woman for sex.

My favorite movie as a child was *The Parent Trap,* the 1961 original with Hayley Mills, Maureen O'Hara and Brian Keith. Early on, I turned to movies to give me a sense of what the world was like outside my family. My conscious self didn't identify the deep connection — the children in the film wanted to get their divorced parents back together. As an adult, I have watched the movie and sobbed. Even the 1998 remake with Lindsay Lohan, Natasha Richardson and Dennis Quaid can turn the faucets on for me. I yearned for a stable family.

Even toward the end of her life, Mom encouraged me to call Dad, to go see him. "If anybody can reach him, it's you."

"Reach him?" I asked. "What does that mean as pertains to Dad? Reach him how? Reach him for what?"

SCENE SIX

Blossoming in the Desert

I crawled out the bedroom window and ran away to Aunt Nini's
— just two houses away because I had to assert my objection
to this move. It didn't work. What was happening?
Had I lost my grip as boss of the family with
the addition of this new stepdad? California?
How could I stop this? What good could happen
so far away from everything I have ever known?

— DIARY OF A 12-YEAR-OLD BRENDA

It was 1960 and my life was about to blossom in junior high and high school. I could see the path ahead and how my road might diverge from my family's. I finished my seventh-grade year at Evansville's North Junior High, played the female lead in the school musical, *Johnny Appleseed,* and dreamed I would continue there through high school and be a star — never mind I had already committed to being a Southern Baptist missionary. For now, I could be a star. But that summer, Herman convinced Mom a move from Indiana to California would offer job stability in the aircraft industry.

All five of us children — from Bill, age fourteen to infant Vivian — packed into one car with Mom and Herman for the trip. Our car was *not* a station wagon. Mom cradled Vivi down on the front floorboard near her feet. The other four of us fought over back seat real estate. Questioning arrangements like this never occurred to me — that's how we lived. I know we didn't stop at hotels, motels or campgrounds. I suppose we stopped occasionally for Herman to sleep because he was the only

53

driver. I don't remember. Dirty, tired and grouchy, we arrived in California after 2000 plus miles in four days for the start of my eighth-grade year.

Our first house in Torrance, California, came in exchange for our service as janitors at the church next to the house, not a bad house except for the cockroaches. We cleaned the church toilets on Saturday and sat in the pews for worship on Sunday. The next year we owned a home for the first time *ever* in Palmdale where we stayed three whole years. We purchased two homes in the same neighborhood — must have been some misguided adult plan to make money on them — and moved back and forth between them during those three years. Those were "the stable years" of my childhood. California, and Palmdale in particular, seemed to lack the yoke of poverty we wore across our young shoulders in elementary school. Could owning a home make that much difference? Herman's steady job? All new relationships? All of the above contributed to my perception that life was better in Palmdale.

Now, a city of 150,000 people, Palmdale was only a town of 11,500 when I started high school there in 1961. Near the infamous San Andreas fault, Palmdale boasts the strange desert beauty of tumbleweeds, prickly pear blossoms and sunsets like I had never seen. Herman — and eventually, Mom — worked for North American Aviation, the major industry of the area. Palmdale sits 2655 feet above sea level — high desert where the days burnt the bottoms of my bare feet and the nights cooled down enough to tolerate living there. We experienced two seasons: summer and winter. Winter gave us snow in the mountains for sledding, but summer gave us 100-plus temperatures on a regular basis. By the time my family got home from school and work, free newspapers of green and orange tossed on our lawn were bleached white on the section facing the sun. I learned to love the desert not because I liked tumbleweeds and cacti, but because I found a village there willing to raise me. Teachers, church leaders and even employers nurtured me through my high school years. Once again, the community around me rose to the occasion of rearing me.

Because this first-ever-home was not ready, our intended move-in date shifted forward two weeks. So we lived in a motel room for the start of school: two adults and five children. My first day of high school began with breakfast cereal in the park. Of course, we lunched at school, but why do I have no memory of dinners during that two weeks? I'm sure we ate some. Mom cleaned rooms at the motel to help pay our tab and argued with the rest of the maids about whether soap already used by others cleaned itself and therefore was okay for us to reuse. We did. We didn't die of disease.

The financial stability Herman provided offset his violent temper and churlish disposition *most* days. Mom allowed him to spank us on a few unforgettable occasions. I still tense up at the sight of a man's leather belt folded in half. I no longer felt proud of his big muscles after the sting of his strap. However, Herman and I maintained a relationship of mutual respect much of this time.

"Dinner's ready," I shouted to the sibs. "Mom and Herman will be home any minute. Ashley would you please set the table?"

Ashley came into the kitchen and noticed the macaroni and cheese. "Oh, no, not mac and cheese *again!*"

We either didn't know about or couldn't afford help from Kraft, so sometimes I got the cheese sauce right and sometimes a yellow sandy substance not intended for human consumption emerged. No one taught me to cook; I just cooked. But Mom's cooking didn't taste much better.

"Don't whine, Ashley. I think it's a good sauce this time," I defended.

Mom and Herman drove up and entered the back door.

"Mom, she made macaroni and cheese again!" Ashley cried.

Mom dropped her purse and her shoulders as she made sure her "piti-ful mask" was in place. "Could I please get in the door and relax a minute before one of you starts bellyaching?"

"I'm doing the best I can, Mom. The kids have their homework done, I trimmed their bangs and dinner is ready." I said.

"I really don't care what you fixed. Get in here and eat — all of you," Mom responded. Tired, depressed and overwhelmed before she got out of bed each day, Mom could not be cook, homemaker, mother and wife while working a full-time job. So we muddled along during those years with my cooking and my child-raising being the best our family could muster.

"Mom, I'm going to a sleepover at Sherry's house Friday night, okay?"

"Sure, just remember if we don't get some things done around this house on Saturday, it never gets done during the week. Get home at a reasonable hour Saturday morning." Mom replied.

I dragged in at the "reasonable hour" of ten the next morning think-ing I was playing the role of the responsible one. But I was bleary-eyed and exhausted from lack of sleep. At no age have I been able to forfeit sleep and certainly not during those teen years.

"You didn't go to sleep all night, did you?" Mom asks.

"No, but I'm home early."

"I told you we had a lot to do today. You know how much I depend on you. You act like you're so willing to clean and shop, but it's really just 'lip service.' You say you love me so much that you're willing to do any-thing, but if a sleepover comes along, you totally forget about me," she accused and started to cry.

"I'm sorry, Mom. I really will be okay today with all we have to do. I can get the bathrooms done, the vacuuming and help with the grocery shopping. I promise. I promise."

Her crying turned to sobbing and a thought sprinted through my brain that something else might be wrong, but the thought didn't linger; my guilt did. She wouldn't do anything to me, like punishment. She really didn't have the authority over me, but she would pout all week and I'd feel like I'd shit on Christmas. If only I had had the wisdom of age to know about such maladies as premenstrual syndrome, mood swings and depression. But I didn't, so I beefed up my role as the good daughter and hoped I would be enough.

Though Mom often held my emotions hostage, she could also model a generosity of spirit we all admired. Before Mom worked for North American Aviation in the blueprint crib, she worked the lunch counter at Woolworth's. One day a young woman sat at the counter and looked at the want ads in the local paper. Mom initiated a conversation and learned the young woman had come to our small desert town to hide away during an ill-conceived pregnancy after which she planned to give the baby up for adoption. Mom brought her home like a lost puppy to live in our three bedroom home which already sheltered seven persons.

"Wow," I reacted. "She's really going to live with us? Since she's a hairdresser, will she fix my hair? And she cooks?"

"We'll see," Mom said, "For now, we need to clean out one of the bedrooms for her."

I didn't question Mom's generosity; her big heart was the best of who Mom was. We sheltered this young woman for the next eight months. She helped me cook and she styled our hair. She fixed Mom's 'do every morning before Mom left for work and taught me how to handle mine — quite a gift for a nerdy high school junior with thin, curly hair.

ൟ ൟ ൟ

Living in California did not cure the need for Grandma's grace — for Mom or for us kids. Perhaps Mom's depression fueled her homesickness, too. The middle-of-the-night taxi fares of years past looked cheap in comparison to train tickets to access Grandma. Putting together the pennies necessary to transport a mother and five kids on the train challenged us regularly. But Mom, who could romanticize most any circumstance, taught us to love the train ride home — home being St. Louis or Evansville, wherever Grandma lived. We liked the Grand Canyon Line because the route through the states that divided us provided excitement and beauty. On one trip, I helped Mom convince my younger sisters they had already eaten when our packed lunches as well as all money were gone.

Finally, the conductor walked through and yelled, "St. Louis! St. Louis! Everybody off for St. Louis!" Mom and I couldn't wait to tell Grandma our stories about no lunches and the delay out west one day that caused the train line to provide a free meal in The Dining Car — a first class experience for a band of ragamuffins.

At 15 feet long, Grandma's trailer — we never heard the term mobile home — was the smallest in the park. So she and step-grandpa Whit agreed to rent the shortened lot adjacent the above-ground septic system. She claimed she never smelled what others avoided. I tried *not* to smell the stench because I wanted to be in sync with Grandma, but the odor crept into my nostrils within minutes of our arrival and didn't wash out until days after we left.

With Mom and five kids in this tiny trailer, Grandpa stepped on someone every day as he left for work. He yelled, "This place is wall-to-wall people!" We didn't care what he said. Grandma's sense of play, comforting lap and need for adventure overshadowed a grumpy grandpa, cramped quarters, train rides without lunch and smelly septic pipes.

Grandma died my senior year. My perception of Grandma was naïve in adult, worldly terms. She seemed to me the perfect human being, full of love without judgment. The halo effect of her love outshone the fact that she was imperfect like the rest of us. She married two alcoholics, remained uneducated, uninformed and wildly co-dependent before I knew that meant crippled relationships. My adult understanding of Grandma's foibles does nothing to change my memory of her as beauty without pretense, adventure without fear, creativity without restraint, security without a price tag — the very essence of grace.

❧ ❧ ❧

I had learned at an early age that I performed well at school. I soaked up the notion that education could buy my ticket out of poverty. School, with few exceptions, created a refuge — a glorious island of organization and positive experiences in a sea of disarray. With positive feelings about education, and in spite of attending 14 elementary schools, I blossomed in high school. Still shy and insecure, I functioned well in class, in several extra-curricular organizations and with a small group of friends. A boyfriend told me years later they called me the "shy Univac." (For younger readers, the Univac was the first significant iteration of a computer.) Those years constituted the beginning of my desire to find my own identity in the midst of family disorder and the realization that the task would prove difficult. Although shy, I performed well in music and theater. Although good at school, I didn't have a self definition of being smart. I didn't know who I was or that I had a choice about who I could become.

Religion formed the only piece of my identity and my life that rested on a firm foundation. In spite of the fact that religion as I had known it was judgmental and narrow. My junior year, I was nominated for a local beauty pageant and dreamed of the crown being placed on my head. I certainly wasn't a beauty. I didn't have a self identity of being pretty, but my music teacher nominated me and I guess every young girl wants to be a princess of some sort. When one of the judges read that I intended to be a Southern Baptist missionary, he asked, "Then what are you doing in a beauty pageant?" I didn't understand why the two demanded separation. I still don't.

During those same high school years, a co-worker of Mom's chastised her because she kept me from attending high school dances. Mom replied, "Hell, I don't keep Brenda from dancing; she keeps *me* from dancing!" Mom called me "the little ramrod" because of my prudish demeanor and posture. From my early elementary school years in Indiana at Grace Baptist Church and continuing through high school in California, I bought into the theology of the Southern Baptists in ways even my Mom didn't. In fact, Mom didn't think about or question theology until later in her life. She attended church off and on during my growing up years — most regularly during my high school years — those three "stable years" in Palmdale when we attended church as a family. Church leaders, not parents, influenced my religious formation. I accepted the role as keeper of the family morals — I use the word morals here by intention because what I learned at church did not form my faith or spirituality. It was moral rule keeping. Don't drink. Don't smoke. Don't dance. Don't go to movies. Some women never wore slacks or shorts and some just never wore them to church.

I suppose some of my prudishness could have been rebelling against Dad's rampant immoral behavior. Wife Number Six, Betty, entered his life as secretary at Sims Brothers Construction Company, which he owned with his brother Charles. I learned on a visit back to Evansville during those high school years that Dad provided her with money for an abortion because he wanted to get back together with Mom. Who knows the truth of the statement? I do know there was rarely a time

Mom and Dad didn't talk even though he seldom talked to us kids. Betty had the abortion, but Dad ended up married to her anyway. They had no other children together.

❧ ❧ ❧

A dark night. A parked car. A lonely road. Sixteen years old and in love, I thought, for the first time. After a few innocent kisses, my boyfriend placed a foil wrapped condom in my hand and said, "Let's go all the way." That's what we called *IT* in those days.

I bolted upright in that car shouting, "Are you kidding? I'm going to college!"

He burst into laughter. He didn't understand what one had to do with the other. In my mind, the two fused together. Poor girls who got pregnant remained poor and too often remained uneducated. The message that education bought my ticket out of poverty and to a sense of self-worth included no layover for sex. Years later, when I saw the movie, "An Officer and a Gentleman" starring Richard Gere and Debra Winger, the dilemma of the local girls resonated with me. The young women in the lower-class area near the naval base received a strong message they could marry a naval officer to escape their poor circumstances and the dead-end town. More often the reality turned out to be pregnancy and abandonment by the sailor rather than being carried off by Richard Gere. I felt compelled to make sure that did not happen to me.

I suppose being a 21-year-old virgin at the time of my first marriage, *in the Sixties,* means I need to thank the Southern Baptists for moral rigidity. Another thanks might be due because I got through high school *and college* having tasted alcohol only once. Had I experimented more with sex, drugs and alcohol, I would not have had the skills and knowledge to handle them well.

Another message that sank in and served me well was that I could accomplish goals through work — really before I was even old enough to work. My brother Bill and I sold 99 boxes of chocolate Sperry Easter eggs to raise money for his Boy Scout troop. We won the prize — a large *chocolate* bunny. Can you imagine how many of those chocolate eggs we had already eaten? We also won tickets to the Barnum and Bailey circus — a big deal! We sat in Roberts Stadium in Evansville a few rows up on what would be behind the basket in a basketball arena. I sat there with my turquoise Easter dress scrunched up tightly in my hands because my stomach ached from too much excitement.

What does it say about girls in the Fifties that my next memory of work also stems from helping my brother with his job, not my own job? Bill had a paper route in downtown Evansville that I helped him deliver on a regular basis. Making our last delivery to the projectionist at the movie theater became a ritual because he let us stay and watch the movie in the balcony. Was this the beginning of my love of movies and my use of them as a window on the outside world?

One Christmas season, with darkness descending early, Bill and I got separated from each other, perhaps because we left the theater at separate times. I can see the ink-stained tears rolling down his face as he made the phone call to Mom and reported, "I've lost Brenda!" Bill was probably infuriated that he had to spend one of his hard-earned dimes on the phone call. My face, no doubt stained with printer's ink too, burst into a smile when Mom and Billy found me waiting inside a store on the darkening street. Other than mishaps of getting lost or fighting with each other, we thought nothing of a ten- and 12-year-old delivering papers downtown. I developed a willingness to work that served me well.

Even Dad helped form my industrious nature. I didn't see him much during my high school years in California, but one summer, I returned to Evansville. I stayed with Grandma Sims and worked as a waitress at Helen's Restaurant where Grandma cooked and grew locally famous for her dinner rolls and pies. During a long day off at Burdette Park, I swam and hung out with friends and sun burned my lily white body. But when it was time for my shift, I put on the stiff black nylon uniform made to torture sunburned waitresses. The next afternoon, I lay in Grandma's front bedroom coated with lotion and tried to find a position that didn't hurt so much. Dad came in to see me, sat on the edge of the bed, examined my sunburn and showed *real* compassion for my dilemma. He said — out loud — in real words, "I'm proud of ya girl for goin' on to work your shift last night." For a blissful few moments, I forgot how much the sunburn hurt as I basked in his approval. His empathic comment may seem commonplace for dad-to-daughter encouragement — not so for us.

Babysitting in junior high and high school always provided some money of my own. Having cared for my sisters since age five, I had the necessary skill, and teachers and neighbors trusted me. Working the snack bar in high school also gave me pocket money. Palmdale, our high desert town, had a winter season, but the snack bars opened to the outdoors for walk-up purchases. I saved and saved and saved to buy a mohair sweater, the fashion must-have that year, and then let it get too close to the electric heater in the snack bar. Mohair smells rancid when it burns. Painful lesson learned: working to buy your own clothes also meant taking good care of them.

Although Mom assigned me the role of achiever in both work and school, ironically, she did not aspire for me to attend college. Her dream for me did not extend beyond graduation from high school, beauty school and a career as a hairdresser. While I did show early interest in hair and makeup, I would have been inclined toward smacking a client who didn't accept what I thought to be her best style. My sassy mouth would not have been a good customer service model. Mom later said the reason I rejected the drugs, music and/or peace movement of the Sixties was that I had blinders on about going to college. Nothing mattered to me as much as graduating from college. Sometimes she really understood me.

As during The Gypsy Years in Evansville, my high school teachers in Palmdale picked up much of the slack of supporting me in the quest toward my goals and even the day-to-day-ness of life. My gym teacher drove me to numerous physical therapy appointments for a damaged elbow. Did she provide this service to all students? How did she know I would not have gone without her assistance?

My science teacher, Richard Turk, taught me that even a good student didn't get to bend the rules to suit herself. I knew I would be leaving for our Christmas trip to Indiana a day early, so I waited until *after* the break to hand in a term paper due the last day *before* break. He knew in a nanosecond what I had tried to pull and lowered my grade for the shenanigan. He and his wife later gave me a graduation party at their home.

Mom and Herman had decided to leave Palmdale right before school started my senior year. Once again, I threw a tantrum. "You'll have to bury me on the steps of Hart High School if you make me move," I threatened.

"Okay, you have one day to find a job and a place to live. Get out there and do it."

Walking the dusty desert roads at the end of August — we had few sidewalks in Palmdale — challenged my bull-headedness and my body, but I refused to give up until I landed a job at the local drugstore. Relief and gratitude rushed through my overheated body. I guess the dust trails of sweat rolling off my face did not disqualify me from running a cash register and dipping ice cream.

My strongest mentor in high school was my music teacher, Mark Darrington. Mark and his wife took me into their home my senior year when my vagabond parents moved on. He negotiated with my boss at the drugstore for my schedule to be adjusted around opera rehearsals for *Amahl and the Night Visitors,* in which I played the vocal lead.

Mom returned to Palmdale for the night of my graduation. She didn't fit with the rest of my high school memories. She wasn't there the night I sang the lead in the opera. She wasn't there for my senior prom. But she made the effort to return for graduation. Held on the football field, the ceremony came to a close, and we all headed to meet family and friends. Before the ceremony, Mom and I had made no plans to find each other — guess we thought meeting up would just happen. But she never found me in the crowd of 438 students and their families. I went on to a party, and we never saw each other that night. I guess I felt some regret: I knew Mom wanted to celebrate the milestone with me. But her presence felt strange and almost intrusive. I didn't feel she was part of the life I had created in Palmdale without her and then she wanted to participate in the celebration. At that point, these feelings were fuzzy and ill-defined. I didn't envision how far our worlds would drift from each other as I matured.

My desert years closed that graduation night leaving me with memories unique to the territory. My high school dance team performed at the Hollywood Bowl. For my 16th birthday, my best friend, Cathy Harris, and I took the Greyhound bus to Hollywood for the premier of *My Fair Lady* at the Pantages Theater at the corner of Hollywood and Vine. We ate at The Brown Derby and browsed a mammoth multi-floored bookstore. Cathy persuaded me to buy the scandalous Sixties novel, *Candy,* by Terry Southern and Mason Hoffenberg, to read on the trip back to Indiana. "It will make you so much more sophisticated than your college peers," she argued. I tried to read *Candy,* but even older and wiser Bill could not explain the sex jargon to me.

That summer after graduation, Bill and I drove together from Palmdale to Evansville in a 1953 Ford. *I am saddened by the fact that I have no idea where Bill was my senior year and why he was back in Palmdale so we could make the trip together — and now he's dead and I can't ask. Maybe it was his time in boot camp.* With no money to stop in hotel rooms, we drove straight through. Despite having no driver's license, I persuaded him to let me drive when he grew tired. The trip made great memories, yet when we arrived in Evansville, we didn't hang out together. Our roads forked when Bill joined the Navy and shipped out to Vietnam and I left for college. Never again were we close or even in contact much. I don't think either of us made a conscious choice — no ill-will between us. I simply exited stage left and Bill left stage right. As adults, we were never *once* in each other's homes.

Years later, Mom reminded me with spite or delight that I turned out to be the family member who flourished most in California though I resisted moving there. In the Mojave Desert yellow flowers of the prickly pear cactus blooms with less than an inch of rainfall annually — one tough lady from the wildflower family. Chameleon-like, I took on coloration of the place — the toughness of the desert flowers. Nurtured by teachers, I thrived when away from the stigma of home and extended family. You have to be tough to blossom in the desert.

Brenda Sims

SCENE SEVEN

Separation Begins

People change and forget to tell each other.

— LILLIAN HELLMAN

College Graduation Day. I'm so excited that I forget to breathe during the morning of getting ready. Mom and little sisters Ashley and Vivian arrive to finish getting ready at the little Quonset hut in married students' housing where I live. I have sewn new dresses for all four of us. Ashley and Vivi twist and twirl in their new duds, so happy to be dressing up and going somewhere special. I have no idea how much they grasp the importance of the occasion or how hard I worked to get to this day. Mom waits while I do their hair before I get to her hair and makeup.

"Okay, sit here and I'll work fast. I really really don't want to be late for line up."

"I'm here."

I speed through base, blush and lipstick and finish with eye makeup.

"What is this extra skin on your eye lids and what in God's name am I supposed to do with it to get your eyeliner on smooth?"

"Wait 'til you get old."

"Really, Mom, you've got to stop smoking. You know it's affecting your skin."

I squirt a last layer of hairspray on my own hair, a last layer of mascara on my lashes and we're out the door.

I never pondered whether it was even fair to dress them up and ask them to fit into my world, now so different than theirs. When Mom followed me to college to live in Georgetown my senior year, I don't think she realized our lives had become different. Who follows their child to college?

During my senior year of high school, I applied only to three Baptist colleges, was admitted to all and chose Georgetown College in Georgetown, Kentucky, because of its proximity to Evansville and because Aunt BJ had graduated from there.

Southern Baptists had called me to mission work, and I didn't think I had permission to consider other careers. I never acknowledged the possibility of a link between my call to mission work and my adoration of Aunt BJ — but she was the only college-educated member of my family and she was in mission work. I was 21-years-old before I gave myself permission to be anything *except* a Southern Baptist missionary. The Baptist church revered missionaries in those days. When any missionary came to speak to a local congregation, the church introduced her as a "real live missionary." I don't know whether the assumption was that dead ones could talk or that missionaries didn't return home alive.

Aunt BJ served ten years in Japan (1957-1967) and ten years on the Gaza Strip in Israel (1967-1977). Her service in Israel coincided with the Six Day War, and upon her return, she looked like a prisoner of war: sallow complexion, glazed over eyes and a constant hyper-vigilance. This heroine and role model satisfied my childhood yearning to believe in life beyond the disarray of my family. In spite of my change of plans about becoming a Baptist missionary, Aunt BJ's influence on my life laid a foundation with bricks called education, faith and service. One role model in the family, even if extended family, spoke volumes when I searched for how someone from our bloodline could flourish. While Aunt BJ's childhood varied from mine, she modeled for me that a member of our family could get a college education and live a purposeful life. It could be done. It had been done. Aunt BJ was solid proof.

My choice to attend Aunt BJ's alma mater ranks as the most significant influence she had on my life. While I graduated 10th in a class of 438 students from a progressive California high school, I cared only about finding a Baptist college. My best friend, Cathy, went to the University of California at Berkeley. Many high school friends and teachers asked with shock, "You're going *where?*" But Baptist colleges best formed Baptist missionaries. For reasons that had nothing to do with being Baptist or becoming a missionary, Georgetown proved to be an excellent choice for me. The college and the small-town location provided stability, new cultural experiences, supportive professors and staff, and a more enlightened perception of life and relationships.

When I started at Georgetown in 1965, there had never been a dance on campus. Those wild fraternity boys had *off-campus* dances, and then my sorority staged the first off-campus dance sponsored by *women*. Sin and degradation — my senior year, the first on-campus dance, sanctioned by the college, instigated great controversy among alums, churches and the Board of Trustees. Some aspects of Georgetown culture seemed antediluvian. Another favorite example came from a professor's opening of the sex education portion of a course. In her deep southern drawl, she stated, "Now y'all know kids who been actin' ugly." With serious intent, she referred to premarital sex as "actin' ugly" throughout the entire course. This idiosyncrasy did not preclude her excellence in teaching. She covered a massive textbook in sociology and inspired her students to absorb the material in ways that would improve their lives and careers. Though we college students perceived her to be ancient, she bridged the chronological divide with humor, intellect and a command of her subject matter.

⌇⌇ ⌇⌇ ⌇⌇

Evansville lay just across the Indiana/Kentucky state line but a world away in some respects. I was not prepared for the racism I found one state further south. My naïveté and my mother's finest quality had me believing racism was a historical part of America — not her current status. To call my worldview narrow would be a generous summation. Georgetown Baptist Church split in two prior to my freshman year. The issue: we had saved the souls of African people with our Southern Baptist mission work, but when some of the redeemed black-skinned folks arrived to study at our colleges, the Baptist churches divided in half over whether we could allow them to worship with us. We had two African-American students on campus my freshman year and one African student. They did not attend worship at a Baptist church until the new Faith Baptist Church formed in reaction to this issue. Even during my senior year when the so-called "problem" had been solved, I still had a sorority sister who refused to swim in the Georgetown pools because black people swam in them.

Georgetown's one movie theater in 1965 was dubbed The Dirty Shame. We joked that you had to take two sticks with you: one to hold your seat up and one to beat the rats off. The college's housing for married students which I and several friends would eventually call home, were Quonset huts from World War II. They rivaled The Dirty Shame for most decrepit. You could see the ground through the floorboards of the house.

I never experienced a curfew until I arrived at Georgetown. Prejudice aside, for that time in my life, the structure and culture felt nurturing rather than constrictive. I arrived at Georgetown at the height of the Sixties culture wars, but hippies and drugs seemed to have missed our Bluegrass campus. As the Sixties evolved with Vietnam protests and hippies in bellbottoms, most college campuses rocked out to Janis Joplin and Jimi Hendrix. At Georgetown, we staged hootenannies on grassy knolls and asked "where have all the flowers gone?" A few guys on campus had long hair but the preppy look ruled the day with requisite Villager dresses and penny loafers with hosiery, the scent of Youth Dew cologne by Estee Lauder wafting through the air. When I stopped in Evansville the summer before starting at Georgetown, my childhood friends Christa and Becky Woods took me shopping for my first pair of Bass Weejuns and taught me that they must be worn with sheer stockings. This Southern college look never reached my West Coast high school and looked weird to my eyes against California surfer duds, but I knew enough to trust these girls about dressing to fit in. Fitting in was my *raison d'être*.

The story of one of my high school friends illustrates how I *might* have made other choices if I had attended one of the California schools many of my friends chose. Kathy Soliah, our high school football coach's daughter and a friend through various classes, represented the all-American girl of the Sixties. President of the Pep Club. Ringo Starr fan. Middle of the road family. Kathy went to a northern California college, started her radicalization and has had more than 15 minutes of fame as the person who hid kidnapped media heiress Patty Hearst when authorities found her with the Symbionese Liberation Army. At the time of Hearst's capture, Kathy had gotten her sister, Josephine, and brother, Steve, involved with the SLA. Kathy escaped prosecution at the time by disappearing. She lived for decades under an assumed identity, Sara Jane Olson, in Minnesota. In recent years, Kathy was found, prosecuted and served prison time.

Granted, it's a leap that if I had gone to a California university, I would have become a radical terrorist. But I remember my mother enjoyed saying, "If Brenda had been as hell-bent on being bad as she was hell-bent on being good, she would have been just as good at it."

Financial planning — any planning for that matter — did not appear on any list my family ever created. This fiscal cluelessness extended to my college ways and means. I departed for college with all my clothes in one blue Samsonite suitcase for which I saved and redeemed Green Stamps. Green Stamps, a popular loyalty marketing program, required pasting stamps in books to redeem for products. *Naiveté* played a significant role in my college plans. Every kind of financial aid known to humankind came my way — a variety of scholarships, grants-in-aid, federal student loans and jobs on and off campus. I even had funds for meals and books. My roommates swore that every time I went to my mailbox, a check arrived from some Women's Missionary Union or other church group. I went to college on dreams; others filled in the economic realities. Still, there was constant pressure about money. Insignificant crises like an empty mascara wand could reduce me to tears on occasion.

Transportation back and forth to home (which during my college years, was variously California, Indiana and Washington State) always presented a financial challenge. One Christmas break, I got stranded at the Chicago airport with no additional money, and the airline said I couldn't go on to Washington because I had somehow purchased a ticket not applicable during the holiday blackout period. Huh? How did I get as far as Chicago on it? God bless the airline personnel who decided to have mercy on what he called "a sweet Southern college girl trying to get home for Christmas." At other times, I made the trip between Kentucky and California on the Greyhound Bus which took three days with no stops at hotels. Being afraid never entered my mind — just another reality of life if I wanted to see my family.

Only in retrospect do I realize the moving hither and yon was directly connected to Mother's depression and constant urge to solve her own mental turmoil. She persuaded my step-father, Herman, to move back to Evansville hoping that being near her family would improve her moods. Herman's career success rested in the aviation industry, and his ability to cope plummeted when he tried other jobs in other industries. So they wandered — usually together but sometimes separately — each hoping the other would get happy, while I thrived in college and moved further away from my family.

My sophomore year, funds got tighter than normal. I decided to drop out to fly as an airline stewardess. As a last ditch effort, I stopped by the college Financial Aid Office of Harry Snyder. He questioned me first about affording to pledge a sorority — easy answer there — Aunt BJ funded my dues on a missionary's salary. Then, he gave me the unsolicited and unwanted advice that the guy I had a crush on didn't have any more money than I did. "What? He has captivated me with his blue eyes and has played guitar and sang to me. Why would I care how much money he has?"

Finally, Mr. Snyder selected me on the spot for a scholarship given by Francis Bennett, a Kappa Delta alumna. She wanted a KD who would share her college experiences by writing to her, visiting with her when she came to campus and, occasionally, through phone calls. We kept in touch for many years. Closed doors opened even if at the last minute.

Keeping up with my own fashion expectations stretched me to tears at times. I had few clothes, but they came from decent stores and I liked to think I had good taste. I would put items on layaway at Adrian's, my favorite store in Evansville. Sometimes Aunt BJ would write in a letter from Israel, "Check your balance at Adrian's." She would mail them a check now and then. My junior year roommate, Lynn Burga (now Bova) wore the same size I did from head to toe. One spring break we went to her house, and in her mom's sewing room hung ten new homemade dresses. Ten new dresses all at once. I couldn't imagine such a luxury. Here's the catch: Lynn had no choice or voice about those dresses. She resented them. Her grudge forged a delightful exchange of my few store-bought clothes and Lynn's larger wardrobe not of her choosing.

Support from unexpected sources continued throughout my college years. My speech choir, The Wordmasters, received an invitation to perform at the Baptist World Alliance Youth Assemble in Switzerland. Funds to go to Europe during college lay far beyond my reach. I screwed up the nerve to ask Dad to help.

"Who do you think you are? *We* don't go to Europe." A two-sentence response from Dad equated to a full-blown lecture. His message rang clear. *Don't get above your raisin'.*

I reported back to my speech professor, Dr. Edwina Snyder, that going on the trip was impossible. She took less than two minutes to respond.

"Meet me at my office tomorrow after your last class. We're going to the bank downtown."

I knew as much about loans at a bank as I did about the physics courses I never took. Dr. Snyder explained step-by-step and personally co-signed for my loan. I floated over campus for days afterward.

At the end of that semester, my fiancé, whose financial means barely bested mine, insisted I forgo the trip to make money for our wedding the following summer. Dr. Snyder again guided me by refusing to allow me to back out of the loan or the large deposit. She knew I would value forever the experience of touring nine countries. Though I have traveled a great deal since, I treasure that first experience of a world beyond my narrow U.S. existence.

I paid off the loan with salary from my first teaching job. I danced with pride the day I made the last payment.

⁓ ⁓ ⁓

Did my parents exist when I was in college? I knew they were out there some-where, but I no longer played a role in relation to them as I had all during childhood. Who were they if I was a young woman on my own?

Dad visited me once on campus. I think. I'm not positive. I wonder if he felt pride I became his only college-educated child. (Much later my half brother, William Dennis Sims, joined me with a B.S. and a J.D. I am so proud of him.) I doubt he thought much about being proud of me. He stayed busy with his own life.

I'm so grateful reality TV series did not exist in the Sixties because

Dad's marriage with Wife Number Seven, Janet, would have made a good one. Janet first appeared in our lives during the short period my family lived in the state of Washington. She was my sister Margaret's friend in high school and brother Bill's fiancé. I'm unclear as to when she moved to Evansville, but when Bill shipped out to Vietnam, Dad stole his girl and married her and they produced half-brother Justin. No, I did not make this up. Bill's version insisted that he dumped Janet in Evansville far from her home and that Dad stepped in. I can't help but wonder if Janet will ever tell her Truth. Of course, their marriage didn't last long, and Janet moved back out West with little Justin. In 2009, Justin found all of his half-brothers and -sisters through genealogical research on the Internet. Now we are Facebook friends.

Since college consumed me at the time of this soap opera, I heard news of the changing relationships on trips "home" but kept my distance geographically and emotionally. Dad's seventh marriage gave me no reason to regret the ever-widening gulf between my family and me.

My junior year at college, Dad fell from a three-story scaffold and pulverized most of the bones in both feet. His recovery stretched out before him long, lonely and painful. To get away from the boredom of his second-floor apartment, Dad threw his wheelchair down the steps then worked his way down step by step on his butt. He rolled himself over to The Super Inn. All day long, Dad listened to Hank Williams, Little Jimmy Dickens and Faron Young and got plastered. In this drunken state, he started his trip home. Happy and drunk, Dad rolled toward home until the wheelchair stuck on the railroad tracks — with a train coming. He told this story on himself and relished the part where he wiggled the wheelchair loose in the nick of time.

The scaffolding fall must have tapped some paternal vein deep inside him that I hadn't known existed. He sent money for me to come home (Evansville, where he lived) to visit him.

Wow, I say as I open the envelope with the money in it, *Dad must really feel bad if he's sending me money to come home. Too bad I can't go this weekend or the rest of this semester.*

I can't say I'm proud of this, but I spent the money on a navy blue pleated wool skirt from Seymour's, my favorite little Georgetown shop, instead of visiting him. In retrospect, I realize this action was a bit passive-aggressive. We never discussed my change of plans; such a conversation would have required more intimacy than Dad and I ever achieved in our relationship. Did I hurt his feelings? I never knew. Was I justified in this one act of rebellion and selfishness? Maybe. What I do know for sure is that there wasn't enough relationship between Dad and me to cause me to have lingering guilt.

Mom existed, too, while I was away at Georgetown — in Evansville, Seattle, various California cities, Indianapolis and finally in Georgetown with me. The summer before I left for college, we had one of those mother-daughter moments when her guidance coulda/shoulda/woulda made a difference to me. I dated a guy that summer who looked wild and handsome and rednecky all at the same time. He rode a motorcycle and I rode on the back from Evansville to Henderson, Kentucky one night as if I had been doing such crazy things all my life. Another night, he stood me up for a date. As I got ready to go out with him the next time, Mom remarked, "The guy stands you up and you're going out with him again?"

"Sounds just like something you would do!" I shot back to her.

For the first and only time, she drew back her graceful long-fingered hand and slapped me hard across the face.

I guess when she had given up her power decades ago, violence may have seemed like the only arrow left in her maternal quiver as her 17-year-old daughter prepared to do something stupid.

Mom hung out there somewhere in my life — always. I knew she loved me and was proud of me. I loved her. My sophomore year, Mom worked as a waitress and sent me her tips. Others may think this a paltry gesture since my family paid not a penny for books or tuition, but that money provided loving support for everyday expenses and I needed the help. My three siblings at home could have used those tips.

One summer, I worked at a book bindery in Indianapolis — my memorable brush with true blue-collar factory life. I stood all day at the back of an industrial sewing machine that stitched the spines of books. I separated one book from the other as they came through the machine and stacked them on a pallet. All day long. Exhausting. Boring. Tiring. Boring. I don't remember a single new or useful skill acquired working there. I marveled at how foolish the young women at the bindery seemed because they dreamed of marriage to a guy at the plant who would "take me away from here."

"It's good for you to experience how 'the other half' lives by working there." Mom said.

Did she think I had no experience being poor? Then I realized it was more about the kind of work she had always been forced to do. Was she really saying I want you to understand what my life has been like? I feel sad that Mom's life never came close to using her skills and intellect. I wish I had said, "I know you have had to work many positions with no choice about them. I'm sorry your life has been full of those meaningless jobs."

My siblings muddled along when I left and could no longer play my designated role in the family. All three younger sibs have acknowledged that I served as their mother-in-fact and that when I left, significant changes occurred in the quality of their lives. Yes, I felt guilt because I passed them on to Mother's care, but I committed myself to the notion that college needed to be the next step in my climb out of poverty and our family tumult.

On one of my earliest visits home from college, I brought to Margaret,

Ashley and Vivian, the wisdom of my freshman experience. I have a clear picture of how pontifical my manner was when I sat them down to receive my knowledge. They were probably thirteen, eight and six.

"There are three paths for getting out of our family dysfunction: therapy, religion and education. Choose one and follow it."

They looked up at me with respect and admiration, but they had not a clue as to how to follow through on my advice. And I had left them to our mother's care.

I now know the journey out of poverty requires all three and more. Back then I thought one of those paths would have them on their way to wholeness and happiness. Ha! Unfortunately, they chose none of the paths — perhaps because I suggested them. Rebellion against my authority figure status? Their respect and admiration for me went only so far. Have they healed from the wounds of our family? I wouldn't say so; maybe they would. At last count there were 17 marriages among the five siblings; this does not include at least three long-term relationships not formalized with marriage, but two of which produced children. A pretty good data point for proving a broken system. Of course, five of those are mine and I'm supposed to be the one who got away from the crippled family. At times I might have qualified for the most damaged of all the siblings but there aren't really any measuring sticks for the emotional scratches and dents and the fractures from life circumstances.

You don't get to choose your parents. Poor parenting is generational. My parents didn't know what they didn't know. Alcoholism is generational. My grandfathers on both sides of my family were alcoholics. Poverty is generational. Not every child born into poverty will possess the skills, tenacity, intellect and other personal attributes necessary to overcome it.

WARNING: To all those who decide to help family members on the road of surviving and thriving, your family will not send you a thank-you note for trying to manage their lives. You won't receive gratitude or praise that *you* got better, healed and became a better you. As I turned to therapy to make sense of my family's problems, my knowledge and experience felt threatening to others. Atop my volcano of shame about family lay a vast dusting of guilt like Mount St. Helen's ash. I could hear the subtle rumble of anger that could erupt from any one of my siblings at any moment and spew all over me — not so much for what I had done but for who I was becoming. Telling the story of family craziness and secrets caused even greater distress. Family secrets should be, well — secret.

My brother Bill charted his own path, too. While I continued to be nurtured in college and enjoyed a life away from our family, Bill garnered nothing but trauma in Vietnam. After returning home from Vietnam, he went AWOL and hid behind parked cars on our dark street when the police came to pick him up. Mom turned him in because she feared the consequences of his being AWOL. Alcoholism defined Bill's life for decades. He inherited the family alcoholism like rich kids inherit the family silver. Sadly, I had nothing in common with a brother with whom I shared blood and history. I can count on one hand the number of times we saw each other as adults. I don't know his children or grandchildren and he didn't know mine.

⁊ ⁊ ⁊

Decades later, through her career, my sister Margaret met Georgetown alums from my college days. She reported back to me with a chuckle, "Bren, your self-image does not fit with the image your classmates at Georgetown had of you — at all!" The people she worked with perceived me as pretty, popular and very self-assured. Ha! Yes, I had friends and sorority sisters in the pretty, popular crowd but in my mind, being part of such a group had nothing to do with me. I certainly wasn't pretty. My self-image still needed development, and I felt college friends saw the surface and didn't know I was poor white trash underneath. I was a good actress. I played the role of preppy sorority girl well. I didn't, however, understand when and where and how my role-playing would morph into reality. At some point, some role would no longer be an act; I would just be me. Will I know it when it happens?

Georgetown opened more cultural doors than I had the capacity to imagine. Although I had exposure to excellent choral music as a high school singer, Georgetown taught me appreciation for all classical music. I walked through the music building and stopped outside practice rooms to hear some virtuoso put in hours at the piano. I never minded required chapel or convocation — okay, maybe a few times when I hadn't had enough sleep — because as the proverbial sponge, I soaked in arts and culture I hadn't even realized I thirsted for.

Christmastime on the Georgetown campus rendered me weak in the knees. The music, the decorations, the anticipation of exams — I didn't discriminate; I loved the transcendent, the exquisite and the drudgery. I had found my home. I left my biological family's home, wherever home happened to be, the summer before my senior year of high school. With the peace I found at Georgetown, I completed a physical and psychological move that allowed me to make a life of my own. Although Mom would follow me to Georgetown my senior year and later to Frankfort and Lexington, our lives always had a gulf that was never bridged again. I suppose she followed me to grasp at whatever security I offered. It was never enough to heal the deep wounds from her own childhood.

In retrospect, I realized my college days were the first time I got to act my own age, instead of a role life had thrust on me. Yes, high school permitted some age-appropriate life, but I always went home each afternoon to the role of mother and caretaker. The campus atmosphere and faculty expected me to be a college kid, nothing more: no requirement to run a household or care for siblings, just be a student. This freedom from family mayhem tasted as sweet as the bourbon balls I also discovered in those years. My Georgetown years were the lowest grade-point average of all my educational endeavors, but the work I accomplished during that period made up for my earlier life and the lack of culture, class and intellectual exchanges, and was the start of relationships of depth and longevity outside my family. I learned what it meant to be my own age, to be middle class and to focus on myself.

Education punched my first and best ticket out of poverty.

The gulf dividing my world from my family's had started years earlier but graduation day widened the distance, which grows to this day. After graduation, Mom followed me from Georgetown to Frankfort where I taught high school. I continued to contribute to my siblings' care with sewing, shopping and haircuts. And if I had a nickel for every apartment I decorated for Mom, I would cruise aboard the Queen Mary. The term "decorate" for what we did seems funny now, but then the "homemaking" made Mom and my little sisters feel better.

During my first year of teaching in Frankfort, Mom and I were shopping in Kroger and ran into parents of one of my students. They struck up a conversation, and I stood and chatted for a few moments. When they left and we went on with our shopping, Mom observed, "Brenda, the way you talk to people is embarrassing. You are so proper and yet overly dramatic. I can't really put my finger on why, but you sound phony to me."

I've pondered her comment through the years and thought about the ways in which I relate to others. What caused Mom to react with surprise and disgust? After college, I began functioning in, speaking to and interacting with a segment of the population Mom had never been part of. Throw in some Southern gentility and no wonder she perceived my speech as phony. My tone and style was foreign to her. The gulf widened.

Act Two

SCENE ONE

Writing My Own Script

"Why do people get married?"

"Passion!???"

"No, because we need a witness to our lives. There are a billion people on the planet, what does one life really mean? But in a marriage you're promising to care about everything, the good things, the bad things, the terrible things, the mundane things, all of it, all the time. Every day, you are saying your life will not go unnoticed, because I will notice it. Your life will not go unwitnessed because I will be your witness."

— MASAYUKI SUO from the movie *Shall We Dance?*

With the maelstrom of my family behind me — so I thought — I assumed that creation of my own kin would constitute the best part of adulthood. Nothing prepared me for a reality in which the formation of my own family would be like a blind woman buying art. I doubt I am the first and quite sure I won't be the last person to come out of a dysfunctional family who thinks she will form the perfect family and "do everything right." In spite of failures and everyday bumps along the road, I cherish marriage and parenthood as pieces of life that have helped me survive and thrive.

At first blush, five marriages would indicate I failed at doing everything right and that I'm not good at marriage. *Au contraire*. Okay, Okay, I certainly didn't do everything right as planned. But I have had two great loves and two marriages that have satisfied and fulfilled me, one ongoing. Another two husbands should have remained dear friends, not husbands. Now don't let me off the hook of responsibility for my role in constructing the less-than-desirable marriages because I had no model for how to craft a stable marriage. Marriage number three, a monumental disaster in judgment also taught me valuable lessons. I discovered more about myself from each marriage, perhaps lessons my parents should have taught me. I grasped more about myself in the good marriages, but I also digested a few morsels from the bad. With time, therapy and additional self-understanding I have forgiven myself for the mistakes. I now embrace the marriages as part of the journey to find myself, know myself and esteem myself. Understanding as relates to men in general did not come easily for me. I didn't have what psychologists call a "daddy hole," the emotional lack of relationship with your father; I had a Daddy Crater and I learned to fill the crater in unhealthy ways.

SCENE TWO

This Must Be Love

Nobody told me the truth about change
How the shedding skin leaves a scar
As I rise from the flames of another seasons change
Touch the earth as I reach for a star
My book holds the memory of every cocoon
Every flight, every time that I fell
And nobody told me how hard it would be
Growing up, letting go, seeing clear
living true to myself

— BETSY ROSE from *Climbing the Rainbow*

Dennis Jay Forintos and I met at Georgetown College in 1968. He had already served in Vietnam and had been exposed to Agent Orange which later caused multiple sclerosis and death. We dated my junior year. My senior year he proposed and I accepted.

With the wisdom of hindsight, I realize marriage to Dennis in 1970 was motivated by graduation from college in 1969. I finished at Georgetown, my home of the last four years. I couldn't and wouldn't go home again, and most of my college friends were getting married. I had a very limited view of the options open to me as a woman. Marriage appeared to be the next logical role. My Southern Baptist moral rigidity may have contributed to the decision to marry. I was a 21-year-old virgin — in the Sixties. I convinced myself, *"This must be what being in love feels like. I really like Dennis, so this must be It."*

I don't have sweet memories of college dates and falling in love. Dennis took me ice skating for our first date. My ankles were so weak, I never

got the skates upright all evening; my lack of ability and interest should have been a clue I didn't have much in common with this long-time hockey player. Later, on our honeymoon, I got another clue when Dennis wanted to ride horses. I disappointed him when the 2000 pound horse fell and pinned my leg under the animal. Athletics and outdoor activities surely would not provide the glue for this marriage.

The summer Dennis and I were to be married, 1970, I moved home to Evansville. Mom and Herman lived there again, and I wanted to spend the summer working and planning our August wedding. I waitressed at a downtown hotel and worked as cashier at a nearby grocery store. The latest rental house for the family sat next door to a funeral home, but we didn't care. I walked in, took charge and tried to make the house presentable.

I prepared a card table and a couple of boxes covered with tablecloths to display wedding gifts Dennis and I had already received: silver serving pieces from sorority sisters, engraved and shining bright and china and crystal that I registered for at the downtown jewelry store in George-town. In retrospect, showing my gifts in that manner seems like trying to display Britain's crown jewels at Wal-Mart. My feet in two worlds were exposed in a sad, pathetic way. The sadness was not a condemnation of my family's poverty, but rather my piteous attempt to make us other-wise.

That was the summer, Herman beat me until I had a blood clot in my leg and I moved to Michigan to get away from my family. Stunned by the impact those events had on my wedding, I later allowed Mom to persuade me that Herman should walk me down the aisle for my wed-ding. I regret that decision to this day. At the time, he represented my better option in the pretense we were a normal family. Decades later I understand the power of denial. Then, I did not understand that deny-ing he beat me and pretending he was a beloved stepfather didn't make it so. My biological dad sat behind Mom and Herman but played no role in the ceremony. My sadness about the decision was not because Dad deserved to walk me down the aisle but rather that Herman didn't, either. I craved an unbroken family and had painted an enchanted wedding in my brain since childhood. This occasion would not be the last time my desire for a whole family and a magical wedding clouded my judgment.

 celo celo celo

One year after our wedding, 1971, Dennis became suddenly paralyzed on his right side. There were earlier signs. During the year we dated, our campus doctor had warned me that "something" serious was wrong with Dennis. I brushed his caution aside. Now, we finally had a diagnosis: multiple sclerosis. After this first severe attack, Dennis' deterioration progressed more rapidly than the normal trajectory of MS. We had no idea how fast the disease would take him. These were not unhappy years, and only in retrospect did I realize I wasn't *in* love with Dennis. I loved him and thought I would take care of him for the rest of our lives.

I began my professional life teaching at Franklin County High School in Frankfort. I taught speech, theater, often the step-children of the English department, and English courses as needed. Teaching felt like slipping my size six hand into a size six glove. I accomplished my best work in teaching with gifted speech and theater students but also with advanced English classes. I struggled with lower-level English classes and misbehavers. Inspiration was my answer to discipline, and if I couldn't inspire them, I faltered but worked hard.

My prudish upbringing left me at the mercy of more worldly and clever teenage boys. When playing a game in English class, I asked the teams to name themselves. One team chose the name "Nads." I innocently wrote "Nads" on the board as they began shouting, "Go, Nads!" Several minutes later — yes, I needed several — to digest what they had pulled on me. Equally clueless about the effect a young teacher in minidresses had on the high school boys, I drove our 1957 Chevy convertible in to the school parking lot every morning, creating their dream with car and teacher. I learned a great deal about young men in those five years.

I agreed to have my advanced drama class participate in a program the guidance counselor wanted to try with a small group. One activity consisted of affirming a positive characteristic you saw in each class member. Since the counselor asked me to participate, my turn came to receive the affirmations from my students. Independent of each other, *ten out of twelve* identified in me some variation of persistence: stick-to-itiveness, never give up, up for the challenge, tenacity. In my mid-20s then, my self-knowledge still developing, I gasped that the outside world, especially my students, knew this about me. I knew I persisted on tasks and why I felt I had developed this capacity. I didn't know the trait paraded around evident to others. In the coming year, I would need all the persistence I possessed and more.

Dennis and I wanted a family, in spite of his diagnosis, and made a strategic decision to get pregnant, layering parenting roles on top of our budding careers. Our son Sims arrived August 13, 1973. His first year of life, Sims spent many evening hours in a car seat or baby jumper on the stage at Franklin County High School while I directed afternoon and evening play rehearsals. Dennis could not care for him alone, and we had no funds for a sitter.

Dennis worked at the Kentucky Department of Epidemiology and I ran our home. Every morning I got *Dennis* ready for work (combed his hair, brushed his teeth, drove him to work) and cared for Sims. By the end of the school year, 1974, friends carried me out of my classroom when I collapsed. The stress had taken its toll on my stamina. Someone needed to be left standing to care for this child we chose to bring into the world. Dennis couldn't. His deterioration accelerated after Sims' birth. He used iron crutches to walk and needed amplified care himself.

During this same period, Dennis' anger at his disease set in. One evening before I was due at church for a musical performance, Dennis could contain the rage no longer. He dropped his iron crutches, lifted our antique pedestal dining room table and attempted to throw the full object at me. The table, a minimum of 75 pounds, barely left the ground, but I knew his endeavor depicted the heavy weight of anger and sadness Dennis carried as this disease took his strength and virility.

A bare thirty minutes after this episode, I appeared at church to sing. I walked down a big staircase in a hooded tan cape with fur around the hood and bottom as I thought, "These people looking at me, admiring my outfit and poise, have no idea what goes on backstage in my life." This was my mid-20s; I had perfected the theater illusion that everything going on backstage stays hidden.

Another evening during this period, Dennis and I played *Password* against another couple. The opposing team husband said on the first clue, "Brenda." The wife guessed, "Sassy." *Wow, I had no idea my sassiness produced such a strong perception she could get the word on one clue!* As with most young people starting out in marriage, I still needed to learn a lot about myself. Unfortunately, Dennis' severe illness at such an early stage of our marriage taught me — once again — I knew how to survive. But those years did not allow me the security to examine and heal the wounds from my family of origin or the luxury of getting acquainted with my whole self.

Dennis and I made the difficult decision to separate in 1974; he went home to his parents in Michigan so they could care for him. I moved to Lexington with Sims. Of course, my family followed, but at first only my sister Ashley, who lived with Sims and me while she attended high school and helped out with babysitting. I agonized over not being enough to care for Dennis, Sims and myself. My physician quoted statistics on the divorce rate among couples where one has multiple sclerosis. Those stats provided little comfort. An amicable divorce ensued; the best decision for all three of us. Dennis spent much of the last year of his life in a hospital bed that rotated his debilitated body. We continued to have contact by phone, and his parents brought him back to Kentucky once during those years to see Sims. Dennis died April 4, 1978. Sims was four years old.

My idealized version of how my life would play out as wife and mother took a strong right jab in the gut.

During these months of Dennis' declining health, I also glimpsed the demands of motherhood, especially mothering a child who proved daily he was one of a kind. Sims never fell asleep anywhere but in his own crib when forced to stay there. He seemed to talk on his way out of the womb. His strong will displayed itself early, also. At nine months, I held him and tried to calmly explain and comfort him about not getting his way. He smacked me across the face. At two, I held his little shoulders and said, "You are the strongest little boy I have ever met; fortunately, God gave you to me and I'm stronger." My statement would be tested again and again and again.

SCENE THREE

Now I Get It

He may not have played it exactly as written,
but there was indescribable charm in his interpretation.

— PAGANINI QUOTE USED FOR BART'S FUNERAL CARDS

The summer of 1972, I worked as a cocktail waitress at the Phoenix Hotel's Firebird Lounge in downtown Lexington. I needed income during the summer when I didn't teach, so a friend suggested I make an audition tape for an on-air position at WVLK radio station, which crowned the top of the Phoenix Hotel. In 1972, with women's voices still uncommon on the radio, the station staff said my voice sounded too high. One of the radio staff knew the cocktail lounge on the ground floor needed a waitress and suggested I apply there.

"Are you kidding?" I asked. "I'm Baptist. I've only tasted liquor two times and don't know any drinks except the beer and whiskey the alcoholics in my family drink."

The manager of the lounge, a woman, replied, "I don't care; you have great legs."

The first week I worked, Robert Bartella, known as Bart, came in with his ex-wife as his date. He was six feet five inches tall, a large, distinguished presence. In the early Sixties when he and legendary University of Kentucky basketball coach, Adolf Rupp were both dining in a Lexington restaurant, Rupp tapped him on the shoulder and asked, "Ya got any eligibility left?" Of course, Bart repeated the incident countless times.

"What can I get for you?" I asked.

97

"We'll both have a Drambuie on the rocks."

"A what?"

"Drambuie."

"Say it one more time and you may have to spell it."

Bart next scrambled to ask, "Are you married?"

"Yes." I replied.

"But not happily," he quickly inserted.

Still married to Dennis, I had not yet become pregnant with Sims and thought I had a good marriage. Bart, a financial executive, proceeded to chase me around three Kentucky counties for the next three years before Dennis and I divorced. During the summer I worked at the Phoenix Hotel, Dennis also grew acquainted with Bart. Bart arranged for athletic tickets for us and advised us about our first home mortgage, and they knew each other in a distant way. When Dennis and I separated and I moved to Lexington, Dennis called Bart and said, "Brenda is moving to Lexington and doesn't know anyone there. Would you look in on her?"

Bart, more than pleased to fulfill the request, "looked in on me" more than Dennis had intended. He was *32 years older* than I. He had two daughters, one two-and-a half years younger than I and the other two-and-a half years older. Although, I was flattered by someone of Bart's status paying attention to me, I told him from the beginning that I would see him socially that summer while Dennis and I were in divorce proceedings but that I could not get serious about anyone. And I would date other men before I would consider marriage again.

We saw a lot of each other all summer. Bart wined and dined me at Lexington's finest restaurants. We spent long weekend afternoons at the pool in his apartment complex and met each other's families. While my eyes opened to the vision of dating an older man, they also opened to a new vision of myself as seen through this man's eyes. I knew Dennis and his family viewed me as part and parcel of a poor dysfunctional family.

This new mature man saw me only as an individual. My family didn't seem to be barnacles clinging all over me in his vision. And Bart was the first person in my life who saw me as beautiful. The old saying, "You're only a beautiful as one man thinks you are," suddenly made sense. I was a different woman as seen through this man's eyes.

Finally, the clanging cymbal of love rang for me. Finally, I got why movies and books and songs were written about this thing called love. Love happened to me that summer. I had no idea the power of this emotion — feeling so strong I had no name for it except "Bart." But I knew the love I had for this man could withstand time and whatever bumps in the road might come our way. In those early years, I didn't know this love would enable us to make love with a colostomy bag between our bodies and cry together afterward. I didn't know this love would give me the strength to pack a surgical wound six inches deep into Bart's body. I didn't know his love for me would mean he agreed to have another child when he was 61 years old. I learned love between us meant all these and more.

I exacted a promise from Bart before we married that we would at least discuss having another child when Sims turned three. So when Bart was 61 years old, our Mark Robert Bartella, his first son, arrived on May 7, 1977. Their relationship played like a symphony requiring only two musicians. Bart also decided to legally adopt Sims because he wanted Sims to feel loved by him and be a Bartella.

Bart brought a very carefree attitude about my family of origin to our marriage. When we dated, he kept a diagram of my clan next to his favorite chair in his apartment. "It's the only way I can keep them straight," he said. I think we met Dad's eighth wife, Irene once. I didn't get to know her. Margaret speculated that Irene and Dad founded their marriage on drinking together — a reasonable conjecture. And when Dad meandered back to Mom for marriage number nine, Bart chuckled and didn't attend the wedding in Evansville, but didn't object when I did. In fact, I think Bart only went to Evansville once in our ten years of marriage. He got drunk during the visit and pinched Aunt BJ — still a missionary at the time — on the butt. Probably was a good idea he never went back.

Child abuse became the issue that moved Bart's somewhat detached attitude toward my family into action. Mom and I decided ample evidence of abuse and neglect existed to terminate my sister Vivian's parental rights to her six-year-old daughter Carmen. As an infant, Carmen had been hospitalized when her biological father beat her almost to death because he couldn't get her to stop crying. Vivian's immaturity and lack of maternal instinct engendered the neglect. She didn't appear malicious in her neglect, just selfish. Carmen's biological father, already out of the picture, had given up his parental rights. Carmen began to have the glassy-eyed look of a prisoner of war at age five. Finally, Bart decided he would supply the money, and Mom filed the suit to remove Carmen from her dangerous situation. We soon discovered ex-stepfather Herman (Vivian's biological father) funded Vivian's side of the lawsuit. Maybe motivated by altruism, he probably believed Vivian to be a good mother. I don't know.

As it should, such an endeavor involves climbing steep legal mountains. At one point, we were due in Louisville for a hearing. We needed to make an early morning 90 mile drive on extremely icy interstates, down to one lane each direction. Our presence, though not mandatory, would speak volumes about our commitment to the suit. Mom immediately suggested, "We just better stay home and pray."

Flabbergasted, I grabbed my car keys and sassed back, "You stay home and pray. I'm showing my face in that courtroom today."

Fortunately for little Carmen, the suit terminated Vivian's parental rights — a difficult judgment to win. Mom was given full custody of

Carmen. In later years, however, Mom returned a teenaged Carmen to Vivian. Carmen ran away, and we did not hear from her for years. In 2010, Carmen, then in her thirties, married for the second time and the mother of two, living in Wisconsin, found me on Facebook. My path has never again crossed Herman's. Bart never questioned whether we made the right choice in suing and, yet, never judged me because of my family.

✂ ✂ ✂

Ten very happy, fulfilling years followed before Bart died of lung cancer in 1985. He said we had a "one issue marriage": his drinking about which he warned me, "Don't ever ask me to stop." So I did what I knew best: I tried to dress up the family.

The two-shaded blue stretchy knit bathrobes clothed our little family of four for more years than I had imagined when I made one for each of us. Bart supported my sewing projects because he thought the activities occupied my days and assuaged my desire to go back to work. My Bernina sewing machine, the best on the market, challenged me enough to buy him one more year of a stay-at-home wife and mother — I had already stayed home three years. Then I gave him the ultimatum of law school or another child. He chose to have another child, a wise decision.

The Stretch and Sew store in the Lansdowne Shoppes taught technique for new knits. Matching bathrobes smacked of cutesy to Bart's no-nonsense mind, but he wore his more and longer than any of the rest of us.

For better or worse, too many of the memories of Bart in his robe mix with the sound of ice in his glass followed by streams of rum and Diet Coke. He awakened around five a.m. every morning. Many Saturdays and Sundays, he sat there in his big orange recliner wearing his bath robe, well on his way to drunkenness by the time I awakened around eight or nine.

The crashing realization that I loved this man as I had loved no one in my life sloshed around in my heart with the cruel irony that he was an alcoholic. Dressing the family up in matching bathrobes doesn't cure alcoholism. My mom pointed out that I had remarked about every guy I ever dated, "Something about him reminds me of Dad." Sadly, the only characteristic I could have seen Bart and Dad having in common would be alcoholism.

With the gift of maturity and Al-Anon, I accept and acknowledge how I enabled Bart's alcoholism. In the beginning, I denied his drinking was alcoholism. Even when he embarrassed me deeply by showing up at events more than a little inebriated, like the night I was being honored as a nominee for Outstanding Young Woman of the Bluegrass. How could he? The drunks I knew didn't dress in coat and tie and go to work every day as successful executives. By the time I knew in my bones he was an alcoholic, I loved him and thought my love would make the difference in his drinking. Foolish love. When he bought rum by the case, I meticulously loosened the state seal, poured out a third to a half and refilled the bottles with water. I deluded myself that I had made the difference when "the issue" went away the last two years of his life. A more accurate explanation: The change occurred because he knew when he retired that he had to either quit drinking or die. Sadly, he did both.

No Ph.D. in psychiatry is required to diagnose that my marriage to someone three decades older than I had something to do with the "daddy crater," but such an explanation presents a shallow interpretation of this deep and rich relationship. Some folks said Bart was my Svengali. He said, "I just provided a stable marriage and home life so you could blossom as you desired." After his retirement, he joked that people in our home town began to know him as *Mr.* Brenda Bartella. Other folks called me his "Trophy Wife," a summation accurate only in the sense that I was the young and glamorously dressed woman on his arm. Marriage to Bart offered me options I had not considered as roles for me, not just glamour girl, but also volunteer civic leader.

I relished the trophy wife moments all the while knowing I could never be defined by such a narrow role — like the strapless shirred white evening gown which Bart called "the Rita Hayworth gown that stopped the gaming tables in the Monaco casino." On vacation in Monaco, we decided to walk through the gambling casino before dinner. Because of the celebrity culture of Monaco such a distinguished older man and *much* younger woman could only mean that they must be famous. As we walked around the perimeter of the room, the gamblers stopped their games and stared at us as if we were the newest *People* magazine cover. In moments like Monaco, I pinched myself and asked, *"Am I still Brenda Sims, the poor white trash girl from the projects?"* The answer to the question even after marriage to Bart remained, *"Yes, I am Brenda Sims and I have grown into a sophisticated young woman who still has a good deal of growing to do in spite of a white gown and a trip to Monaco."*

My family joked that Bart thought he chose a glamorous sex object and, in fact, got a Baptist Sunday school teacher. He didn't get one or the other; he got both. The jokes and theories created part of the fun because our marriage rested on solid knowledge of each other. We enjoyed music, spectator sports, books, movies, travel and shared parenthood. Since Bart had peaked in his career, he gave himself permission to enjoy these experiences in a way he didn't allow with his earlier marriage and his older children. Grateful for a third act, he made the most of it.

I do not underestimate the financial impact of this marriage on my life. Bart moved my standard of living from struggling lower middle class to secure upper middle class. I remember the first time I thought, *"I don't have to parcel out the strawberries because there are enough for all of*

us to eat as many as we like." I remember when Bart directed me, "Buy diapers in large quantities when they go on sale." I had never had enough money to buy more than the quantity necessary short term. Upon seeing an advertisement in the paper about a scissors expert demonstrating at McAlpin's Department Store, Bart suggested I run over there to buy several different kinds for our household use. Specialized scissors? The height of luxury to this girl from the projects.

Bart provided a lovely 5,000-square-foot home, swimming pool, constant travel and even after his death, paid for my two master's degrees, Mark's undergraduate degree and Sims' long and winding road through education. Bart, of course, had a comment about this financial impact, too: "I know Brenda could walk out of this marriage any day of the week and make it on her own in fine style." The glue of this marriage of broken persons was love.

When I insisted on a pre-nuptial agreement for the marriage following Bart's death, my attorney tried to dissuade me. "Brenda, you are *not* a wealthy woman." He had no idea how vast my inheritance appeared to little Brenda Sims.

The repercussions of losing Bart in 1985 rippled forth like a tsunami. My relationship with my Mom turned out to be one of the big ripples. Bart had asked Mom to come over and chat with him before he died.

"I'm leaving Brenda with enough money to rear and educate our two boys, but I have asked her not to help support her family members. There are not sufficient funds for reaching out to you all," he explained.

So before his death, Bart bought Mom a new car on which she soon let the insurance lapse. Then she allowed my sister Vivian to drive and crash it.

The most important outcome of this chat between Mom and Bart was that Mom *fully believed* I would not follow through on his request. When I did, she never forgave me. I still have great sadness about this right angle turn in my relationship with Mom. The message I received was, "If you don't take care of me, I don't love you anymore." I suppose what she felt was, "You've taken care of me all your life, why would you stop now."

I was not aware of how I could not let go of Bart. Ten years after his death, a new seminary friend commented, "Since knowing you, I also feel like Bart is just away on a business trip and will be back soon." The mirror she held up for me reflected that I still communicated a relationship with Bart existing only in my heart and mind. For years after his death, I endured nightmares in which Bart still lived but had moved on to another house, wife and family. Stating the obvious, I had deep-seated fears all men would leave like my Dad.

Bart's death blew the foundation of my life out from under me. I knew during our marriage that I most likely would have a life beyond Bart. I lulled myself into believing I had prepared myself for such during our ten years together. How foolish. Issues from childhood that I assumed to be distant memories, no longer part of who I was, reared their ugly heads: insecurity, fear, neediness. *What role should I play now? No longer the glamour girl on the older man's arm, who am I now?*

Dennis's death and my grandparents' deaths ill-prepared me for this new experience of grief. And how was I supposed to escort my little boys, 12 and eight, through losing their daddy? I always expected Bart's death would signal the time when I returned to a career, so I should get busy with building my resume right away.

On the first year anniversary of Bart's death, Sims walked in the house and declared, "Mom, the whole house smells like the day of Dad's death."

Okay, we gotta get out of here.

I loaded up the car, and we headed to Evansville to visit cousins and play for the weekend. Our evening entertainment, a Sally Field-James

Garner movie called, *Murphy's Romance*, seemed innocent enough for our escapism plans. The plot, however, did a sneak attack on my grief as the story played out between the younger woman and older man. I collapsed on the floor and sobbed in front of my boys; they cried, too. One of numerous reminders; there's no way around grief, only through. Art, in most all forms, reaches into my core and releases my feelings. Books during this period had the same affect; *Cold Sassy Tree* by Olive Ann Burns ignited another melt down. While melt downs may not always be conveniently scheduled or polished and performed well like a role, the release of tears and grief and sorrow washes the soul to live another day. I needed and experienced more than a few in the wake of Bart's death.

In 2001, after meeting John, my current and last husband, I saw an advertisement on TV for a new film about a great love story. I thought, *"Oh my god, I'm being reminded of great love and for the first time in 16 years I don't wish for Bart to still be alive!"*

❧ ❧ ❧

Marian Anderson's explanation of life as a black woman in a white world paralleled how I began to feel as a child of poverty, now functioning in an upper-middle-class world. Anderson said, "Sometimes it's like a hair across your cheek. You can't see it, you can't find it with your fingers, but you keep brushing at it because the feel of it is irritating."

When Bart died I was serving on six non-profit boards. The emotional and financial stability Bart provided unlocked my creativity, drive and energy. I became the youngest president of Lexington Woman's Club, the largest Federated Women's Club in Kentucky. As I got more and more involved in volunteerism — circumventing our agreement to be a stay-at-home mom, Bart joked, "You work more than 40 hours a week; you just don't get paid for any of it."

Finally, I rested secure on the giving end of charity. The reversal required some getting used to. The Lexington Woman's Club Clothing Center provided two outfits for every indigent child referred to the Center. I rejoiced that the guideline was "do not send any child out of our Center in any outfit in which you would not send your own child to school," but I had nightmares in which the children clothed turned into my siblings and me. I now understand part of my anxiety rested in being "found out." *Would I still be welcome in the Club if they knew I was "poor white trash?" Was the hair across my cheek visible to others? What would the other women think if they knew many in my family still qualified to send their children to our Center?*

I also chaired, danced and sang in the Follies that funded the Clothing Center. The year I chaired the Follies, I felt I needed to bring perfection to the decades-old event. My theme, "A Touch of Elegance," intended to raise the quality, struck some of the ladies as humorous. Women who had constructed and painted the backdrops for years asked me to stop by one day as they worked. I arrived to find them all hard at work dressed in old prom gowns! We laughed, and I learned that when they gently poked fun at my perfectionism, it brought healing to the curse.

During this same period of volunteerism, I discovered I did not measure up to unwritten rules of the Junior League — in spite of leading the largest women's club in the state. I was attracted to the projects of the Junior League but knew few women in the group. I called the one person I knew.

"Sue, I would like to know more about the Junior League and perhaps join the group."

"We don't work that way, Brenda," she answered. "We are an invitation-only group."

End of conversation.

Rejection by the Junior League translated to my damaged self-worth as re-confirmation I was still a welfare kid. By this time, though, I had matured enough to ask, *"What does this mean? Does it say something about me as a person? What does it say about the Junior League?"* About this same time, I asked an acquaintance if the project she worked so hard on was connected with her Junior League. She looked at me as if I had landed from Mars and said, "The Junior League doesn't take my kind." It took me a few seconds to realize she was Jewish. (To be fair, I think the Junior League policies have changed, officially, if not in fact.)

Another lesson learned. But I'm not sure I fully knew what I needed to learn from this experience; I knew a seed had been planted that I needed to ponder. Was society really on this ladder with some of us higher than others? Who wrote the manual for what merits higher and lower places on the hierarchy? I had some thinking to do.

SCENE FOUR

New Family

The human tendency is to desire answers for our questions,
but what we really need to grow is to surround ourselves
with people who help us raise questions
about our answers.

— DR. MARDY GROTHE

One of the unexpected benefits of marriage to Bart became a relationship of depth, trust and hidden sources of richness equal to a vein of gold in a darkened cave. If everyone we meet along the way can be our teacher, I claim some great teachers who helped me learn from my errors. While I have needed *all* the teachers to help me stay on my path to wholeness, Leah Marie Bartella deserves a spotlight. Leah, Bart's older daughter, had a grocery list of reasons I could have been suspect in her eyes. She chose, instead, to forge a relationship of love between us.

Leah and I met the first Christmas Eve I dated Bart. She arrived a bit early at his apartment to find me in her father's bathrobe, hungover because I was foolish enough to drink *two* crème de menthe cocktails to celebrate my 27th birthday. In spite of all the alcoholics in my blood line, I've never been able to get past the second drink.

With one distasteful experience of a young stepmother already under her belt — Bart's second wife was 22 years younger than he — Leah must now contend with her father dating someone 32 years younger and even younger than *she*. In the 30-plus years since, Leah has delivered a tour de force of grace, integrity, love and honesty. She lives in another state but has attended *all* my weddings, continues to come for holidays, invites us to her home regularly and always comes home for significant life events.

When she came home for Mark's birth, Leah, the baby and I were walking through the grocery less than a week after delivery. Leah was carrying Mark, and I moved out ahead of them concentrating on shopping.

A stranger commented, "Wow, you sure look good for having had a baby so recently." And as a baby, Mark definitely looked more like her child than mine; the Bartella DNA was foremost.

Leah didn't miss a beat, "I'm not the mother. She's up ahead there, and she looks way better."

As years flew by, Bart swore that every time I visited Leah, I came back with a more feminist attitude. She taught me to look at the world from a perspective larger than my Kentucky education and Baptist upbringing. While a committed feminist and peace activist, Leah approaches all of life with a gentleness of spirit that entices others to examine their beliefs rather than forcing or debating the issues. I attended my first peace march with her.

In the Eighties, Leah purchased the historic Chalfonte Hotel in Cape May, New Jersey, against her father's best advice. Some would say the description of the Chalfonte as historic is euphemistic — *old* might be more accurate. Whatever adjectives we chose to put on the Victorian Lady, the Chalfonte became a member of the family. The blessing of Leah in my family doubled with the addition of this old, overgrown house.

Bart and I visited the hotel together only twice, but those sojourns became apocryphal. On our first trip, the staff and regulars were alert and curious about Leah's family, especially this young stepmother. The Chalfonte Dining Room is long, narrow and formal in the tradition of

Virginia gentility. The former owner and her cronies, all in their 80s, waited with anticipation at the "family" table. As Leah, her sister and I walked the full length of the dining room, we could not help but hear the loud but hoarse whisper, "Which one is the stepmother?"

The next evening, we had cocktails on our balcony with this same group of long-time Chalfonters. Ms. Martha Nash, a delightful 80 year old, stretched to reach 4'10". Bart, an imposing 6'5", appeared on the balcony in his Seventies yellow polyester pants and shirt. Martha craned her neck back and examined the full length of him and declared, "If you like yellow, you got a bargain." These two stories and a picture of Bart in the *very* small bathtub in the Bridal Suite kicked off the decades of relationship between our family and Leah's hotel.

After Bart's death, the Chalfonte played an even larger role for Mark, Sims and me. Each of us worked there as staff on numerous occasions and have a deep, warm affection for the place that far exceeds a building even if you call the ancient gingerbread historic. The Chalfonte is a community, an attitude, a tradition and a long, refreshing laugh. Leah brought this gift to our lives.

When Leah arrived in Lexington for the last days of her father's life, she brought with her the woman who became her partner for decades and another beloved member of our family. Cynthia Ann Harris met Bart only on his death bed, but they connected via music, both being trumpet players. Cynthia, a professional trumpeter and composer, played for his memorial service.

On my first visit with Leah after her father's death, she and Cynthia informed me they were a couple. Leah professed shock that I already knew and more surprised when I assured her Bart knew also. In later years, Cynthia and I teased Leah, "You think because you have a paper sack over your head no one knows you are a lesbian." Ironically, as we went through the boys' growing up years and functioned fully as family with Cynthia, Mark was the one who never "got it" that Leah and Cynthia were partners. Mark, our bright and intuitive superstar, couldn't see the forest for the trees. When he was 21 years old, I insisted Leah have a chat with him before someone else told him. He had long been jealous of having to share Leah with Cynthia, but he didn't seem to have a need to name their relationship. Chagrined he never figured out they were partners, Mark became a radical advocate for gay rights.

In recent years, I introduced Leah to a new friend. The friend remarked, "Leah is the kind of person I'm just glad to know exists on this planet." I couldn't have said it better. She has been one of my most valued teachers in this life long task of becoming the person I am intended to be.

SCENE FIVE

Mother

Making the decision to have a child is momentous.
It is to decide forever to have your heart
go walking around outside your body.

— ELIZABETH STONE

The summer my son Sims, then 25 years old, reached the summit of Mount Kenya, I had a profound dream. The room in the dream looked like a doctor's clinic. I, however, knew the place was heaven. Still very much alive, I demanded to know what a recently deceased friend would do in heaven. The white-coated official said, "Don't you understand? Heaven is where we all do what we're best at."

When the official in charge left the room, I eyed rows upon rows of file cabinets and wondered if my file rested in any drawer, though I was still alive. Wild to know what I would be doing when I got to heaven, I sneaked over to the appropriate drawer and found my full name on a sleeve. I took a deep breath and opened the file folder. There — alone in the folder — lay a single sheet of paper with one word on it: *mother*.

Oh boy, did I have a bit to chew on when I awakened the next morning. I would not have put motherhood at the top of any list of what I'm best at. Would my sons have placed maternal skills at the top of my best list? I do remember with crystal clarity one day when the boys and I sat at Arby's on Limestone in Lexington and Sims said as Mark agreed, "Mom, the world will never know or understand what a good mother you were because we were such — uh — challenging children, but *we*

know." They were both in their 20s at the time. You don't get many pay-days like that.

When I became an adult at age five, I related to others with a maternal style, especially my siblings. Granted, my innate personality informed my role as mother: bossy, sassy, firm. When my own children came, I felt confident I could parent them so as to overcome the genetics I passed along to them. I felt sure the rewards of having my own children would surpass the challenges of parenthood by far. I can now say, "*Nothing* I have done in life taught me as much or in the same way as parenting did."

I brought into this world Sims Marshall Bartella (originally Dennis Sims Forintos) and Mark Robert Bartella. My story of mothering them lies apart and above all else in my life. Husbands came and went; my boys and I created a constituency of three members who faced the world together. No relationship in life stretched me more than parenting my first-born son, Sims.

Since a therapist has to be supervised occasionally no matter how long he has been in practice, one therapist we saw in Lexington told us he had more supervision by his colleagues on our case than any he treated. He once stated that when we all came together, he would shake himself and send his brain a reminder, "This is the Bartella family. Stay alert. Be sharp. You're going to need all the skills you have."

"If a therapist," he explained, "considered only your story, or only Sims's story, or only Mark's story, each would provide enough thera-peutic mountains to climb. But to layer the three of you in one family, throw in three strong personalities and you have all the tests a therapist could want for an entire career." Sims had buried two fathers by the time we saw this therapist and had ADHD and dyslexia. Mark lost his father when he was eight years old and struggled with significant depression as a child. Another family therapy group we attended called us "The Face Family" in honor of the A-Team guy named "Face" because he was very handsome. They said, "All three of you are attractive on the outside and have so much pain on the inside."

When we lose a parent during childhood or have parents who can't or won't do the job, the subsequent therapy has been called "paid parenting." Among the three of us, we paid for a lot of mothers and fathers.

SCENE SIX

My First Love

Quality time and vitamin C and a book before bedtime at night,
I did everything right,
Then why, when I reach out to touch him, does he hold me at bay?
Something inside of me dies
When I look in my son's shuttered eyes,
So far from here. So very far away.

Tricking and treating and soccer games and the second grade's Halloween show,
I was sure to go.
And yet he is stumbling through jungles of bitterest black,
Lost in the fog that he buys,
Wearing a rebel's disguise,
Unwilling, or unable, to come back.
I never claimed to be the perfect mother.
I made mistakes. Well, everybody did.
But God, I was so glad to be his mother.
And God, oh God, oh God, I loved this kid.
I love this kid.
Patience and laughter and trips to the beach and tickles and song,
Did I do something wrong?
Am I kidding myself? Am I simply rewriting the poem?
Telling myself a few lies,
While somewhere a frightened child cries,
And I wait, and I hope, and I pray that he'll find his way home.

— JUDITH VIORST from *Did I Do Something Wrong?*

No surprise that Sims and I are the survivors of our nuclear family. Whatever gene pool tributary flows through my Dad surely flows through Sims and me, a physically strong current, almost primal. Sims ran on all fours like a Cheetah by age two. Sims, my dad and I can all sit like men do in primitive cultures with the soles of their feet on the ground and knees bent into a squat position. The wiry, white-haired, blue-eyed stripling so like my Dad now hailed from the upper-middle-class suburbs instead of the Ohio River bottom Dad called home, but the genetics shined through.

At six, Sims ran ahead in a darkened theater to take his seat next to a stranger for viewing *Tarzan*. The stranger inquired, "Are you excited about seeing the film?"

"Of course," Sims replied, "I'm related to him, you know."

I should have added, "Not only is he related to Tarzan, he is related to my Dad, Clarence Sims, which is a more powerful force in his life than his relationship to Tarzan." Sims' physicality, personality, perseverance, intellect and stubbornness are legendary but so close to truth as to have legend and truth indistinguishable. In addition to Tarzan and my Dad, Sims is a product of my marriage to Dennis Jay Forintos.

The multiple sclerosis that afflicted Dennis progressed at a rapid pace, but with the youthful optimism of the Boomer Generation, we believed modern medicine would keep the disease at bay. We wanted a child. We inquired about the genetics of MS; after assurance that MS did not have hereditary tendencies, we made an intentional decision to get pregnant. Dennis would have been a great father for Sims. An athlete, a veteran, a thinker, he had so many qualities that would have made for good parenting had his life not been taken by MS.

Dennis and I handcrafted a cradle that rocked on its base for Sims's first bed. When Dennis' weakness or unsteadiness prohibited him from execution of the next task in this project, he directed and I got the job done. Wise persons shuddered at the thought of a skill-saw in my hands, but you do what you *gotta* do. During the same period, while six months pregnant, I changed the oil and air filter on our 1957 Chevy convertible and rotated the tires as Dennis coached from the sidelines.

After 16 hours of labor, my son emerged with a scream and a pink face on August 13, 1973. I fell irretrievably in love with him when the nurse held his slimy little body up for me to see. My first love. My forever love. I knew instantly the ferocity of this love was primal — no limits — whatever necessary. I suppose my thoughts on that day ran toward future challenges like losing sleep, the frustration of potty-training or relentless days of carpooling. I soon learned and relearned that parenting this child would be more like pulling your face off, walking on beds of nails and digging down deeper for strength and resilience that I thought humanly possible. But I resolved that day no challenge would separate me from this first love.

The quirky little cradle we made nestled beside our bed in the first home we owned in Frankfort. At *two weeks old*, Sims made the cradle swing by himself as he threw a temper tantrum because his first formula constipated him. He raised the front half of his body off the tiny mattress with sheer anger. Little did I know how this angry outburst predicted the eruptions to come.

Parenting books didn't prepare me for a nine-month-old who slapped my face or a two-year-old who toddled to the end of the diving board to hear everyone swoon. How many moms remember to tell three-year-olds, "Don't climb on the roof of the house today?" Although an energetic, hyper-alert and hyperactive mother, I despaired at being one step behind in my care of Sims.

Sims' first educational experience was in a Montessori School from three to six years of age. In retrospect, Montessori proved an excellent learning method for Sims. He excelled and learned in his own way. He self-diagnosed his learning disability at five years old, when he announced, "Mom, the other kids at school are taking letters and putting them together and making words and reading them. I know I'm smarter than they are and I can't do that. Why?"

After Montessori School, we applied for enrollment at an excellent private school. His test results so differed from how he presented himself in the interview portion, the school thought they mixed up the files of two children. Alas, they had not. Additional test results began to show the mountains we were about to face: dyslexia and severe ADHD combined with high intellect. We decided at that point to give him another year of kindergarten in a more structured environment to see if maturity would help. It helped a bit, though not enough.

Sims finally entered first grade at our local public school. At this stage, he saw no need to wear the cute little Izod shirts and preppy pants, *de rigueur* in our upscale suburban neighborhood. He wanted to dress as a different film or story character every day; some days wiser heads chose to let him go to school as Indiana Jones rather than stage a battle *royale* over traditional school clothes.

Ms. Meade, his teacher, reported, "When he walks into the room each morning the kids crowd around to beg and wait to see whom Sims anoints as his best-friend-for-a-day. Some even pay him quarters for the honor."

Then one day, Ms. Meade reported, "Sims rocked the class today when he chose Crystal to be his best friend for the day." Crystal was an African-American girl bused in from the projects, who certainly had no quarter to pay him. Even at seven his charisma enchanted those around him.

By third grade, we had tried all manner of intervention to bring Sims' skills up to his age level and mental capacity. Nothing fit his unique combination of diagnoses. When we tried the learning disabled class at public school, he again expressed his opinion, "What am I doing in that class? Those kids are dumb and I'm not." Not the most politically correct or empathetic statement, but accurate to his perceptions. In desperation, we investigated and chose a boarding school for his fourth and fifth grade years.

If there was an Academy Award for parenting stamina, I would have won for having reared Sims. Please note, I *did not say* an award for the best parent or the best result, rather for the willingness, strength, fortitude and tenacity to stick to the assigned task. The duel of wills tested both of us. High school staged the championship bout. After six years, a half-million dollars (no exaggeration), and his documented genius IQ (still no exaggeration), he graduated from high school at the age of 21. The journey included two public high schools in Lexington, one boarding school in Virginia and a therapeutic high school in Northern California from which he finally graduated. Persistence won — at least, if the goal was to get him through high school.

During his high school years, I continued to lag behind Sims in my efforts to think of what he would do next. The *piece de resistance* in the struggle between my *naiveté* and Sims' creativity came when I picked him up from high school in Virginia for spring break. He asked as soon as I arrived whether he could bring a friend home for vacation. I consented and he replied, "Great. Pull around to the back of the dorms to pick us up and I'll help him get his things." We took the child home to Kentucky and began to have a great time — until the phone call came from the school asking if we knew anything about the kid's whereabouts. I had taken another parent's child across state lines and neither the parents nor the school knew where he was. In today's world that would constitute kidnapping but 25 years ago we trusted each other more. How many times did I need to get snookered by this son of mine before I wised up? More than I care to admit in print.

ᘓᖇᓑ ᘓᖇᓑ ᘓᖇᓑ

Labor Day weekend of 1992, I took my problematic, troubled 19-year-old son to a therapeutic high school in the Northern California mountains. The boarding school consultant who recommended The Cascade School to our therapist stated, "It takes a very strong and committed parent to select this school. There are no locks, no gates. Every student stays by choice and that *choice* usually means a parent who has drawn a line in the sand." Our therapist assured the consultant I possessed the kind of strength to tell my son he must stay or be out on his own with his misbehaving ways. The situation demanded I be willing to go to even greater lengths because Sims was over 18 years old and needed to have etched into his brain that this was the end of the line for him *with me*.

We flew into San Francisco, rented a car, drove another five hours to the tiny town of Redding and checked in to a hotel. The next morning, we started the 45 miles up the mountain to The Cascade School. The terrain was serious California wilderness for this urban momma — so intense and unpopulated, I felt quite comfortable peeing on the side of the road when necessity demanded. I felt the continuous pull on the rental car as we ascended the mountains from the town to the school. I also felt the tension in the car: between Sims and me and between every nerve of my body. Immediately upon arrival, Sims was taken on a tour while I spoke with the admissions officer, Ms. Toffelmire. My son soon stormed back into her office; announced he would not be staying; grabbed the car keys and took off in the car with me standing on the porch calling to him.

Ms. Toffelmire and I first called the California Highway Patrol and then discussed our options. CHP counseled that an all points bulletin would not be a good idea because we would not want him caught up in the California court system for a felony: stealing a rental car not registered in his name. I called the hotel and requested they get my airline ticket out of my room and lock it in their safe.

Sims returned to the hotel and I was able to get him on the phone. He declared he would kill himself if I didn't let him return home. My children and I are nothing if not dramatic, but this declaration scared me. At this point, I really didn't know whether he would be capable of taking his own life. He had not made such threats before. I knew going back to Lexington was not an option for him or for me. His drinking, drug use, wild and erratic driving and sneaking out of the house at all hours had to stop here and now. At 19, Sims still did not have enough credits to graduate from high school. I asked him to promise not to do anything until I got down the mountain to talk with him. He agreed.

Ms. Toffelmire drove me back to the hotel. I got so sick at my stomach on the drive down the mountain, I asked if I could drive her car so the motion sickness at least would be abated: there was no relief for the terror in my stomach. I found Sims in the lobby and we headed to our room to negotiate. What followed were hours of talking, arguing, crying, screaming and many phone calls to our family therapist at home. At points throughout the day and in to the evening, he threatened to kill himself, threatened to injure me and made various other desperate ultimatums. I held my ground that he must stay at the school or be out on his own — and out on his own in Redding without even a bus ticket home. As the afternoon wore on, he exhausted all his resources. I felt in my gut he was getting more frantic and reckless and afraid. I was getting more and more scared.

I sent Sims to get sodas and called our therapist for the umpteenth time to tell him I had reached the point of being afraid to stay at the hotel with him. Sims knocked while I was still on the phone and panicked when I didn't answer right away. He too realized this drama was climaxing. The therapist told me to let him in and tell him I no longer felt safe in his presence and I would be leaving, returning to Kentucky, and he would be on his own in California. I repeated the statement and laid the phone on the bed with the therapist listening while I dealt with Sims, one of several times that day I chose to do this.

He started crying and screaming like a wounded animal. He cowered on the floor and screamed until a guest from another room came to check, thinking the voice was a woman being beaten. The guest left, but returned with the front desk manager and a security guard. They informed me I could not check out and leave Sims there because he was too out-of-control. This was not a version of Sims I had experienced before. I knew this moment would be a turning point in his life and mine. I felt terrified of the possibilities for both of us.

I gave him three options: psychiatric hospital, police station or back up to the school. But he was beyond reason. He sat rocking back and forth on the bed or cowering on the floor saying, "Why do I have to die tonight, Mommy?" Yes, my 19-year-old had regressed and was calling me "Mommy."

"Is there a heaven, Mommy?"

"I want to see Daddy, Mommy. Why did he have to die?"

"I'm so scared."

"I can never be alone, Mommy."

During these many hours of conversation, Sims revealed to me in bits and pieces that he had been sexually molested at the first boarding school he attended.

"You don't know what that man did to me, Mom."

Sims had been nine years old when we'd sent him to that first boarding school. Raw terror engulfed my full-grown, pseudo-macho son and reduced him to a cowering trembling little boy. I offered to share the story of how I was sexually molested as a five year old, if he would talk with me about his horror. No deal.

"You don't need to know what Mr. Van Sant did to me."

Now I was thinking I had to get him to a psychiatric hospital in spite of being just as afraid of getting him caught up in the California mental health system as I was of the judicial system. Since he was 19, I had no rights about determining his care.

At 8 p.m., I called the headmaster of Cascade School. I started to tell him about the molestation and Sims yelled, "Don't tell him, Mommy, don't tell him." The headmaster then said to me, "He was sexually molested at another boarding school, wasn't he."

He then went on to explain, "Because of Sims's history and his extreme reaction to being left here — well, we deal with the damage of child sexual abuse everyday. Can you get Sims to listen to me on the phone?"

Incredibly, Sims agreed. I heard him say, "I am not afraid of being molested again, I can take care of myself now, but I can never ever be alone again the rest of my life." The headmaster astoundingly talked him into coming back up to the school and promised him he would not be left alone.

With both of us sobbing, we started our trek back up the mountain at 8:30 p.m. Dark, no road lights, our pitiful rental car wouldn't go over 35 mph at times on the steep road. I felt — as I have felt on a few other occasions in my life — there is *nothing* this world can dish out that I can't live through.

Later that declaration would be tested mightily, but on that night, I thought I was driving up the highest mountain of pain.

As we entered the school property, a fawn walked slowly through the path of our headlights. In the midst of this dark day and darkest hour, we both gasped at the beauty and strength of the little guy.

The school leadership asked me to stay the whole weekend in Redding to be on hand for whatever else might happen. When I finally returned home, I allowed my friend Rachel to read the journal I kept for the whole trip. Her only response, "When they make the movie of your life, will you make sure I get to play myself?"

Sims stayed at the Cascade School for the full two-year program — with one attempt to run away — after all, strong mindedness comes with his DNA. He was vice president of his class and graduated from high school the year he turned 21. He wrote me a note and gave me pictures when he graduated. I have them all framed so I will have a constant reminder of one of the first summits we reached together. His use of "Mommy" in the note harkens back to the innocent little boy he once was, not the scared young man in the hotel who regressed to childhood out of terror:

Merry Christmas Mommy,

By now you have received the rose from me. My other gift to you is me. By this I mean the "me" I became in the last year at Cascade. These pictures represent the childhood version of me and my current state. I have come back to the beginning. Two of the pictures are of me showing joy at two and at twenty. The others are you and me together, happy once again at twenty and how we were when I was two. I have come full circle — my point is my Christmas gift to you this year is me — your Simmies back again.

I love you always.

୦⁊୦ ୦⁊୦ ୦⁊୦

As I browsed through letters I had written to Sims over a period of years, a deluge of feelings swelled, feelings more intense with time. One letter I had written to him after his high school graduation, shattered the logic that I could take a deep satisfied breath, my job as parent complete. Not

so. He was 21 and I parented on, or tried to. As was often the case, I was still trying to teach him responsibility about money. I suspect no parent ever feels finished, but this gig had required such extraordinary effort.

Reflecting on this parenthood, I am struck by how desperate I often felt: desperate for Sims to know I loved him, desperate to somehow, someway give him self-esteem, desperate for him to achieve his dreams, desperate for him to find himself. In other words, desperate to be successful as a parent — desperate for both of us.

Well into his twenties, he stopped by my condo on his way out of town for a beach trip. As previously indicated, he is great fun. His *joie de vivre* rubs off and watching him gives pleasure to all around. On that day, an objective observer could have mistaken him for a five-year-old on the way to Disney World. His excitement so contagious, I handed over my credit card for the trip with specific instructions, "For emergencies only." I had no idea the water being too cold created an emergency demand for wetsuits for Sims and his buddy — a genuine crisis. Did I mention he will tell you, "I can charm the sunburn off a lobster?" And, oh, by the way, he looks like a cross between Brad Pitt and Paul Newman. Whatever clothes placed on his body hang like a GQ model ready for his photo shoot. And as I wrote these words, I realized how often I was both angry with his irresponsibility and proud of him at the same time. His charm has served him well in this world, and my susceptibility to it was a testament to its power and to the blindness of a mother's love.

In response to September 11, 2001, and his brother's death, at almost 30 years old, Sims enlisted in the Marine Corps. My response to this decision:

Dearest Simmies,

The image in my mind since you called with your exciting news has been the little nine-year-old white-haired kid hugging his back pack and saying, "This is going to be the biggest adventure of my life." In retrospect, we know *that* boarding school experience brought both adventure and pain. My prayer as you go away again is that you have lots of adventures and no pain. As we have learned time and time again, mommies can't always protect their babies from pain — therein, lies my fear.

I want this adventure for you! I think you will excel as a Marine and all the pieces will come together in your life. I want you to once again experience that feeling of being the best of who you are and feeling so good about yourself. I don't think the Marines have any idea what a quality, strong, intelligent, leader they are getting — but I know!

You were special from the day you were born; life will reveal that to be true. Remember — "life doesn't make you who you are, life *reveals* who you are." It has been and will again be revealed, that you are an extraordinary young man.

When you went to boarding school at age nine, you and I planted some marigolds along the fence behind the garage at Tally Road. They bloomed all the way until Thanksgiving which was your first visit home. I looked at them many days to remind me of your precious face and that we had planted them together. As you go away this time, I will look at the pictures of our road trip to remind me that there will be other moments to share with you.

John and I are both so pleased to be taking care of Spratley. She, also, will be a constant reminder of you.

In the letter I wrote to you in Africa, I told you that I loved you more than my very breath. That is as true now as the day you were born. I would give up my very breath to keep you safe! I wish it were that easy.

I love you my precious, precious son! Return to me.

Love,

Mom

During Marine boot camp, at five to ten years older than the other recruits, Sims earned the position of Honor Man for the entire class of 600 men. He excelled at being a Marine. He excelled for too long — which may be the curse of being a good Marine or merely the length of the war and number of deployments.

After 39 years, with the help of Al-Anon Family Groups, I am letting go. "Hello, my name is Brenda. I am learning to reconcile the over-iden-tification-with-motherhood with the I've-done-what-I-was-supposed-to-do version of motherhood." I'm learning about detachment in Al-Anon and how healthy survival for me means letting go of the need to protect and mold Sims into what I think he should be. Sims has been "should" on enough.

SCENE SEVEN

Bart's Gift of Love

Love — not dim and blind but so far-seeing that it can glimpse around corners,
around bends and twists and illusion; instead of overlooking faults
love sees through them to the secret inside.

— VERA NAZARIAN from *Salt of the Air*

In one of my favorite photos of Mark, he is standing up holding the side
of the crib in his blue-and-green clown-themed nursery. He was such a
happy baby, we speculated he surely wouldn't be much of an intellect
and feel so happy about the world. Ha! Little did we know of the fierce
mind developing behind his silly grin. He grew into the college boy who
chased professors after class to ask one more question or argue one more
point. That nursery picture hailed from one of the happiest periods of
my life: Mark and Sims delightful at their respective ages of ten months
and four, marriage to Bart fulfilling and life abundant. When Bart agreed
at age 61 that we would have a child, I knew this baby would be a symbol
of our deep love and commitment. What a blessing that we could not
foresee the pain to come.

But the pain of the future was unknown and the joy of Mark's childhood was delight-filled. When Mark started first grade, the longer day
without his nap challenged him. He cried and said, "Why do I have to
go to school all day to read words like hat and cat and bat when I can
already read independence and curiosity?" I put notes in his lunch box
each day to encourage him. I didn't know until years later he saved those
notes into adulthood. At some point, as a young man when he fought

the urge to stay close to mom versus the urge to separate with deliberation, he staged The Ceremonial Burning of the First Grade Notes. *I wonder how the ceremony worked for him. I think he wanted the burning to mean he was grown up now and less dependent on his mother but that independence came years later.*

His elementary and junior high years flowed by smoothly even after his Dad's death when Mark was eight years old. Junior High twisted his world around as he begin to realize he wasn't athletic and he needed a "cool factor." In order not to be labeled a "nerd," he strategized that he would misbehave on the bus because that wouldn't affect his grades and in choir because his teacher loved him so much she wouldn't mete out harsh judgment. Then kids would not think he was a nerd. He got thrown off the bus, made his choir teacher's life hell and still dragged the label of nerd through junior high. He was Student Body President and insisted the principal just thought he ran the school, but really Mark did.

At some point during Mark's teen years, my mother began to realize Mark's personality and demeanor leaned more toward mine than his father's. She did not hide her disappointment and told me so. I laughed. I must admit "parenting myself" may have had a healing quality. I showered on Mark all the attention I craved from my parents. From piano recitals, plays and singing in public, I tensed and tingled as much as he did, knowing the excitement and terror of performing when you're so young. I lived the rush all over again through him. I understood through Mark the sensitivities I had as a child which had to be suppressed in order to survive. I hope I always gave his feelings permission to live and grow; however, I know there were times in our challenging journey that my strength sent the message that his compassionate nature by contrast was weak. *Not so, dear Mark, be who you were meant to be.*

In spite of his adolescent issues, relationship with Mark tasted delicious, and so damn rich as to make you sick afterward but you couldn't stop eating because the last bite tasted as good as the first. I often said, "Mark could annoy a dead person." He would strike an annoying accent or riff on a teenage song and no amount of threats, punishment or isolation stopped him from trying it the next day. But I was also the one who enjoyed his extensive talent for comedy and theater. As with Sims' charm, I found it hard to punish the very characteristics that I found so appealing.

The rock solid foundation of love we held for each other provided a stage upon which we played. We both enjoyed acting and deserved Oscars for our performances as mother and son. I was at my best when parenting him, and he certainly was at his best in being a devoted son. The way we bickered made others nervous and uncomfortable but formed an intimate intellectual joust for us.

An acquaintance at The Chalfonte Hotel in Cape May commented, "I've never seen a mother/son relationship like this!" I don't even know what he observed except Mark, a young man in his twenties at the time, blew raspberries on my cheek in the Chalfonte Dining Room. I recognized our relationship as extraordinary, so I was never surprised others found it unusual. In later years, I learned he admitted to others I was his best friend. His love for me had qualities unlike anyone else who has ever loved me.

By the time he was in his late teens, Mark saw me more accurately than I saw myself. After being present when a group of my friends were over, Mark said, "Mom, you don't get the impact you have on your friends. You don't get that the energy in the room changes when you are there or not there. You don't get that you are the leader in any group you are part of." He was right. I didn't know who I was yet. And even as a teen, he began to hold up the mirror to let me see. The irony here is that I'm not sure he ever credited himself with these same characteristics.

Our closeness also caused me to have blind spots in parenting Mark.

Mark no doubt attended fewer days of high school than anyone who ever graduated. During those years, 1991-1995, the combination of his clinical depression and smoking pot created an insurmountable lethargy. Mark excelled at inertia and stubbornness. If he thought what I wanted him to do was breathe, he would find a way to stop his very breath. He would get up and drive his buddy to school and drive back home, sneak into the basement and sleep all day. When told he should be a stand-up comic, his response was, "Hell no, that's too much work. I'll be a sit-down comic." I spent years coming to an acceptance that Mark was hurt by his child-hood. Like me, he was overly sensitive to his environment, but unlike me he didn't have the blinders on so the only goal he could see was college. I ached that I could not "fix" his depression and give him the focus and energy I had to smooth his way to adulthood. I no doubt denied the amount of marijuana he smoked and probably protected him from him-self far too long.

The years of do-nothingness extended beyond high school when he refused to go to college. He tended bar at Applebee's and smoked a lot of pot. When his girlfriend Rebecca's patience ran out, he announced to her, "Wherever you go for grad school, I'll go with you and do my undergrad." He did, and finished college in three years at Sam Houston State University, Huntsville, Texas, just shy of a 4.0 in History and Pre-law.

Mark and I logged hours on the phone during his college years in Texas. Because he didn't find many academic peers at Sam Houston, he would call me at all hours of the day and night, oblivious to my sched-ule. Most always, I was so pleased to talk with him, I didn't mind. I was also willing to admit my boundaries with Mark were not always wise ones. He thought it imperative that I debate constitutional law with him at that very moment. When he had worn me out, or long afterward, he would say, "Now I'm calling Bazz, (Bazz Childress, our dear friend closer to his intellectual peer and a conservative) so I can argue the other side of the issue." Delight that Mark had reached this level of excitement over college motivated me to stay on the phone long after patience ran out.

I saved an email Mark sent to me while in college. It started with the now ubiquitous Marianne Williamson quote:

Our deepest fear is not that we are inadequate
Our deepest fear is that we are powerful beyond measure
It is our light, not our darkness that most frightens us.
We ask ourselves, who am I to be brilliant, gorgeous, talented and fabulous.

We are children of God.
Our playing small doesn't serve the world.
There is nothing enlightened about shrinking so that other people won't feel
Insecure around us.
We are born to manifest the glory of God that is within us.
It is not just in some of us; it is in everyone.
And as we let our light shine, we unconsciously give other people
Permission to do the same.
As we are liberated from our own fear, our presence automatically liberates others.

And Mark's email response to the quote:

"Pretty inspiring, huh? I see much of myself in her words. I think you exemplify her ideas. You have inspired me my whole life and I thought you should read this and know how much I love you. You have power beyond measure, and, as a manifestation of God, liberate me.

P.S. Read it to Sims."

Motherhood brought me more joy and taught me more about myself than any other relationships of my life. I didn't know the degree of my strength until my children tested it. I didn't know the charm I possessed until I saw it in my children. I didn't know the extent of my ignorance about money until I tried to teach financial responsibility to my own children. I had to dig deep to hone my skills, define my values and communicate in ways I hoped would create healthy, balanced, contributing adults.

The creation of my own family forced me to think about what I did and did not want to repeat from my family of origin. The degree to which the ghosts of my childhood lived in my house surprised me, bit me in the butt and their words escaped my mouth when I least expected. I learned to be vigilant. I had to name and accept the impact of bad role models so I could recognize them when they popped up in this new family I created on my own. I had extraordinary raw material with which to work. But I found out the hard way, parents are not the Creator.

SCENE EIGHT

Still Trying

I think we all wish we could erase some dark times in our lives.
But all of life's experiences, bad and good make you who you are.
Erasing any of life's experiences would be a great mistake.

— Luis Miquel

I offer no excuse for my part in this gigantic mistake. Devastated by Bart's death and desperate for emotional security, I thought I found a good man. A college professor who attended church, had two sons of his own and cared deeply for them, Dan shared many of my values and desired the kind of home life I wanted for my boys.

My therapist pointed out to me that after losing Bart, my life was like a building broken down with grief and years of wear and tear. I felt I had to hurry up and build great new additions professionally and relationally when I really needed repair work. Ahhh, hindsight, you fickle teacher. I had already tried one job since Bart had died, assistant director of the Opera House in Lexington and found my children needed me more than I needed the job. So I returned to what I did well and what flexed with my children's schedules. I began work on a master's degree in communication at the University of Kentucky, a brilliant solution professionally: get more education while the children grow up.

My planning regarding marriage didn't show as much patience. I irrationally thought two and one-half years were enough time for my grief, which verifies how grief cripples your judgment. I had not done the work in therapy that would have made me comfortable being single and alone.

I was still desperate to fill that Daddy Crater. I wanted to be married again — now. I underestimated the psychological healing I had yet to do. I remained clueless concerning damage I still carried from childhood wounds. I didn't know the work that still lay ahead of me. I didn't know what I didn't know.

After a couples bridal shower, shortly before the wedding, my groom-to-be, Dan Moore, commented, "Your friends seem to think of you as being very sexy. I'm not comfortable with that."

Was it the joke gifts? Sexy lingerie from showers? Where was this coming from? Why now? I had no answers, only questions.

"No kidding." I replied. "Did you think you were the only one on the planet who had noticed?"

Then a few months before our wedding, Dan stopped by my house after work. He always looked ill-at-ease, but that day something was bothering him. He shifted from foot to foot and finally said, "Brenda, don't you think it's necessary for you to bury Bart's ashes before starting a new marriage?"

"I suppose," I replied. "Haven't given them much thought."

"I'm not comfortable living in this house with part of him still here."

I pondered the conversation and tried to see his point of view.

Was I ready to bury Bart? Did that small box in the closet mean more to me than I was willing to admit? But the wedding is so close. Everything's planned. Everyone's so excited for me. I can't think about this too much. Dan's just insecure, and I sure can't fault him for that, I've been insecure most of my life. I can see how it might be the fair action to take for him.

I remembered that fall day I picked up Bart's ashes from the crematorium. The air had that change-of-season smell that indicates everything is dying. With Sims and Mark in the back seat, we drove home in silence. How do two little boys, just eight and twelve, make sense of their Daddy being in a box? Oh, God, I don't want to relive that pain and I don't want to stir the grief for the boys, either. I just want to be happy. Planning this wedding is such fun. It's my dream wedding.

After discussing the burial with Leah and her sister, we agreed it was time to let go. They both made plans to come to Lexington. The cemetery grounds are beautiful regardless of season. It was damp that day, but the first blossoms of spring peaked through. My heels sank in the soft dirt as we walked toward the small tent. My friend the Rev. Ken Bailey said the appropriate words, and we placed Bart in the ground. Each of us dropped a handful of dirt.

Dan attended the service. The boys and my step-daughters didn't seem to mind him being there. Were they accepting his presence just for me? I know they wanted so much for me to be happy. I felt myself staying detached from the entire process just for Dan's sake. I could play any role if I made up my mind to do it.

Okay, since Bart's ashes were no longer in the house, surely, that would be the last of the conversations about my previous marriage.

A few weeks later, Dan and I were lounging at his townhouse, enjoying a few hours without children. I wanted to discuss wedding plans every day, all day. I was good at event planning, and this was my big event. Every detail would be exquisite. Dan couldn't or wouldn't focus on the wedding plans that night. Finally, he said, "Brenda, do you really think it's appropriate for you to keep all those journals you wrote during your marriage to Bart if you're moving on to a new marriage?"

I tried with little result to keep my indignation out of my voice. "Those journals are a history of my life, my story. There are positive and negative memories in those journals. They're not about holding on to memories of Bart."

"Well, it feels to me like you're not letting go of one marriage before starting another one."

"Stop it, Dan. You can't wipe away my history. I loved Bart. He's dead. I'm marrying you." Was I pleading, trying to reason? If I could just keep my voice steady.

"I would just feel better if you got rid of them," Dan said.

I turned silent. Days passed. I thought the issue had dropped. The wedding date grew closer.

"Brenda, are you going to get rid of those journals or not?" Dan inquired.

"Really? I have to throw away years of journaling to make you feel okay? Is my commitment to marry you not enough? How can you be so threatened by a dead man?"

I was alone in the house on a cool April day. I gathered the journals together — small notebooks, large art paper books, spiral-bound, hardbound — eleven years of my life. I took them to the family room fireplace, placed them on the grate and lit the match. I sat and watched as the flames glowed, soot and sparks flew into the chimney and, finally, the grate lay bare except for the slight evidence of fanned pages, charred chunks of my life. I put my will aside and buried my own ashes. I don't know what motivated me to follow through with his request — denial of my own feelings for sure. But now I could get back to my wedding planning.

I wasn't thinking; I was reacting. Reacting to Dan's insecurities with insecurities of my own.

Finally my wedding day arrived. On a sunny June day in 1987, my precious Mark and Sims, ages 10 and 13, walked me down the aisle of a packed Central Baptist Church to start the wedding of my dreams and the marriage of my nightmares. Many folks had moist eyes as they watched our smiling trio. Everyone celebrated my marriage to this young, good-looking professional man because they also had watched and prayed as I lost Bart to cancer.

My white satin dress caressed my body from shoulders to knees then blossomed into a train that followed us to the alter. The sheer bodice gave just the right hint of sensuality. Sims and Mark looked handsome and grown-up in their black tuxes. My five bridesmaids wore rich emerald green satin and carried tropical bouquets that hinted of the Hawaiian themed reception. The groom appeared nervous but handsome, and the service went smoothly.

The gorgeous wedding to Daniel Allen Moore ended, and the doomed marriage began. For the record, *no* family members and only *one* friend voiced misgivings about this match. Even my therapist later apologized that he had not noted the signs in Dan of — what? Mental disorder? Dysfunctionality? Woundedness? All of the above? His issues with sexuality and obsessive-compulsive disorder and irrational thinking escalated from the honeymoon until the day our divorce finalized. Perhaps I should have read more into behaviors like paying a licensed electrician to rewire a friend's house after Dan had already done it. He was a professor of electrical engineering; he knew that wiring was correct. But his obsessive thoughts would not cease until he paid to have his house rewired by someone licensed.

On the honeymoon when he brought up issues he had not mentioned in a year and half of dating — all issues related to his need to control me, such as what I wore, where I could go and who I could be friends with — my stomach knotted in fear.

I remember looking out the balcony of our Hawaiian hotel on the peaceful beach scene below. We were getting ready for dinner when Dan asked — out of context or relevance, "Remember that night you were late coming home from choir practice? Where did you go? Were you with anyone?"

"We were engaged already. I was committed to you. Why do you need to bring this up now? What do you need from me?" I replied.

"Well, why won't you take my last name then? Are you still in love with Bart?"

"Yes, I still love Bart. Dying doesn't make you stop loving someone. But that is my past, you are my future."

My expression in all the honeymoon pictures looks like I'm gritting my teeth. I was. I recalled in those days in idyllic Hawaii, how he had assured me months ago that he found it "necessary to rake back the glitter when confronted with someone who shimmers like Brenda."

I had replied, "You're doing the job with a goddamn backhoe, not a rake."

The warning gong should have clanged long before it did with concern over his unhealthy attitude about sex, relationships and more. I knew Dan had lingering issues about race, not surprising for one who grew up on a farm in Alabama, but these issues strangely conflated with sex. He had to carry a note in his wallet to stop obsessive thoughts that I had slept with the African-American man who replaced my driveway. While I'm not opposed to a relationship with an African-American man, I didn't know that particular man except for his ability to replace broken concrete. After the first six months of marriage, Dan's thinking began to anger me. I squelched a daily urge to say to him, "Do you have applesauce for brains?" I comforted. I cajoled. I had sex with him after arguments because he needed it. There was a connection with sex that I didn't understand.

Another of the difficult issues in 18 months of marriage surrounded the issue of humor. Dan had no access to humor, and my boys, now ages 11 and 15, and I survived on ours. Flatulence is a sacrament to adolescent boys. Dan denied he ever experienced such a human function. Mark would lay in wait outside the bathroom door and scream at the top of his lungs if a sound similar to passing gas emitted from behind the door. How can you refrain from laughing? One therapist pointed out to Dan that the boys and I also laughed at ourselves, which he seemed incapable of doing.

Mark impersonated Dan in *Saturday Night Live* style. Although very well built, Dan bore the unfortunate characteristic of a high waist. In a culture already pushing pants to the lowest possible place on the hips, Dan's high waist supplied a perfect set-up for caricature. Mark would pull his pants up to his armpits and imitate Dan's overly serious mode of speech. I tried on most occasions to play the adult and refuse to laugh at these impersonations. I threatened dire consequences if they didn't cease and desist. Laughter often won. To be fair, the scorecard in this new family was always three against one.

The marriage lasted 18 long months. I learned an important lesson about myself from this marriage: I had very low tolerance for someone who needed to control me in order to feel safe himself. The concessions I made, such as burning my journals, became lessons well-learned. Circumstances had necessitated I become my own authority at an early age. In the final analysis, he didn't stand a chance of controlling me in my 40s. I also learned I didn't possess enough relationship skills to bridge the psychological divide between Dan's dysfunction and my own.

め め め

After the short and misguided attempt to work at the Opera House, I resolved that raising two challenging boys needed to be my focus for another few years. I developed, however, what I dubbed Business Monday Syndrome. Our local paper carried a business section on Mondays and a short column always noted, with pictures, people who received promotions, moved to new positions or companies or received awards. Every Monday the guilt, expectations of self and general depression swept over me. My carefully laid plans called for the role of successful professional after Bart's death. The stay-at-home-widow role didn't fit any ideal I

had of myself. I did enjoy extensive volunteering during this time, building a network that served me well later, but the itch to "get on with the show" calmed down only with the next degree and a new career path.

In between marriages three and four, I finished the master's in communications and started a professional speaking career. One of my professors at UK recommended this path given the full picture of my skills. The job fit. The speaking engagements coincided with my gift for performance and suited my Miss Know-It-All self who had been in charge since age five.

Mark asked, "Who wakes up one morning and calls themselves a professional speaker? Mom, that's who."

I marketed myself locally based on relationships from living and doing volunteer work in Lexington. My business flourished with what the corporate world considered human resource related topics, such as self-esteem, work and family life balance, stress management and time management. A hot trend in National Speakers' Association, an early Nineties nod toward info-tainment, was singing along with your speaking. So I opened and closed keynote addresses with songs. Audiences of that decade ate it up.

In spite of this career success, I longed for a serious, stable relationship with A Man. The Daddy Crater demanded to be filled.

ෂ ෂ ෂ

During this same period, I also began to question all I ever knew and believed about religion, Christianity and spirituality. Though not everyone who explores spirituality will view disproven teachings and conservative doctrine as betrayal, I did. Literal interpretation of Jonah swallowed by a whale, the Earth created in seven 24-hour periods and a literal resurrection of Jesus' body rested heavy on my psyche as lies told to me by people I trusted. Around age six I had asked my Sunday School teacher,

"How do Christopher Columbus and Adam and Eve fit together?"

"They don't," she replied and moved on with the activity.

The message I received was "don't question what we teach here at church."

From age six through my college days, I was too busy pleasing others, especially teachers in school and church, and getting out of poverty to be bothered with theological reflection. Some of these teachings, I rejected subconsciously during my college years. Others clung to me like my poor white trash background, polished over but beneath the surface. Early teachings, like one's early environment, hang on until you replace them with something new. The Asparagus Tips Sunday School Class at Central Baptist Church in Lexington became the first group of people with whom I questioned the old and, more important, developed a new theology that continues to renew with every year. The folks in the Asparagus Tips class were friends with whom I had been building trust. One person who would play a more significant role later was Jim Herbert. These people were intellectual seekers who would lay out new ideas and offer each other a safe space and the freedom to accept or reject them. They were the first group of people who taught me that religion and spirituality could grow deeper through questioning.

I'm also indebted to the Rev. Kenneth Bailey, a minister at that same congregation, for introduction to Dr. Wayne Oates' book, *Struggle to Be Free*. A spiritual memoir, Dr. Oates' writing gave me permission to reject and throw off a Christian role that no longer fit. Dr. Oates also had to find a path out of poverty. I'm finally over my anger at the churches of my childhood. Maybe. Kinda. Sorta. One of many areas where I practice giving the forgiveness I have received for years.

However, many more passed before I enrolled in seminary to discover what I did and did not believe.

SCENE NINE

Shoulda Been Just a Friend

You can't fix what's wrong with you
trying to change other people.

— DR. MARDY GROTHE

Loneliness and longing for companionship caused James Glenn Herbert and me to mistake our great friendship for love. I do love Jim to this day. But as a seminary professor who knew us both said, "Whatever made two intelligent people think this marriage could work?" Loneliness and longing, that's what.

Jim and I began our friendship in the Asparagus Tips Sunday school class of Central Baptist Church, a silly class name for a group of people who considered their willingness to dispute theology with each other the best part: the tip of the asparagus. The depth of study and questions appealed to both of us and opened us up to each other. The Asparagus Tips class was one of those steppingstones that helped me reach a point of trusting friendships. Jim attended seminary and needed to complete an assignment on the use of the Genogram. He asked me to be the test case or faux client for the project. Our meetings to input my family history into this Genogram project produced the beginning of our dating relationship.

According to the GenoPro website,[†] the Genogram based on family systems theory, is a pictorial display of a family relationships and medical

---

[†] http://www.genopro.com/genogram/

history. The instrument goes beyond a traditional family tree by allowing the user to visualize hereditary patterns and psychological factors which punctuate relationships, to identify repetitive patterns of behavior and to recognize hereditary tendencies.

Jim asked, "Would you be willing to use your family for a class project I have to do on the Genogram?"

"I'm game." I replied. "Oh, buddy, do I have a family system for you!"

The assignment directed us to ask a question (as a therapist would) that needed resolution in my life. I told Jim, "We'll have to make up one because I'm in such a good emotional space about my life; I don't have any problems needing answers right now."

The question I concocted for the Genogram was genuine, I just didn't know why I needed to answer it. In light of the grief and turmoil I had lived through, this question seemed a trivial thing to ask.

The question: "Why, if I have little or no anxiety about public speaking, acting, or teaching, do I sometimes have all-consuming anxiety when I sing publicly? I've had as much or more training in vocal performance as any other skill."

The methodology of the Genogram involves creating a family tree. For ease of illustration, let's say the family tree has circles around all addicts, squares around all abusers, triangles around those who were abused, trapezoids around mentors and so forth. My family tree is a geometry teacher's dream. I filled out the chart and we ended the session.

Jim returned days later. During the casual visit, we were sitting at the breakfast bar at my house on Summershade Court. He gently asked, "Tell me more about the aunt who taught you a song and prepared you to sing in public for the first time when you were five years old."

An electric shock radiated from the top of my head to the tips of my toes. I could barely form the words, "Oh my God, she also sexually molested me on a regular basis that same year."

I have known this fact all my life. The path to the long, narrow, cold bathroom at Grandma's house led between the pot-bellied coal stove and the cabinet where the black desk phone rested, number Harrison 48595. The click of the sliding bolt lock. My aunt telling me to lie down on the towel.

"I was five. I didn't know I had a right to say 'no.' I didn't suppress the molestation. I have felt guilty about the incident all my life. And yet I pooh-poohed the significance of the actions and certainly did not name her actions *abuse* or connect the incidents with singing. I excused her because she was a teenager at the time. I thought her behavior didn't *count* as sexual abuse because she was female."

Jim listened intently as I continued to recall the abuse. "I remember when I was studying voice with Dr. Noemi Lugo in the Nineties at the University of Kentucky. Something she said makes sense to me now."

"Brrrrrrrrrrrrenda," she would say rolling her R's with delight, "you have this beautiful sound you refuse to let out. For some reason your voice seems contained, locked up tight."

"Now I understand when, where and who locked the door."

Shortly after this Genogram experience, I read a newspaper interview with Marilyn Van Derbur, the former Miss America who speaks out on sexual abuse she experienced as a child. I identified strongly and clearly with the feelings described by survivors. I *knew* those feelings. I had already spent many hours in therapy and felt as though I was in a good place at that time. I now had new material that demanded exploration for me to fully know how this childhood abuse might be affecting my adult life. I made an appointment with a therapist to begin again the process of healing.

ᘒ ᘒ ᘒ

During the subsequent five year period, Jim and I broke up and went back together more times than Elizabeth Taylor and Richard Burton and my Mom and Dad put together; we married only once.

One of the more notable breakups occurred after we had sat up until midnight addressing our wedding invitations. Jim arrived the next morning to inform me he had cold feet, was too afraid of marrying again for fear of failure. The humiliation — I did perceive the episode as humiliation at the time — played out in our tight-knit church community. One Sunday after the breakup, Jim hid in the room above the baptistry because he heard I was in attendance. I strutted off to confront him. Our confrontations always resulted in getting back together. Although we loved each other, a thread of sanity in each of us knew the relationship would never work. Neither of us could muster the strength to pull on the thread.

When asked why this marriage didn't work, I resisted what others pointed to as the reason: that Jim and I came from two different economic worlds. I lived a lifestyle of abundance due, of course, to money left to me after Bart's death. Jim lived a life of scarcity due to career choices he had made and perhaps others reasons which I am not able to articulate for or about him. When another of my seminary professors pointed this out to me, I blurted out, "Are you kidding me? Jim comes from an upper middle class family. His father was a university professor; his mother distinguished herself in several areas while being a stay-at-home mother and rearing four children. I'm the one who came from poverty and lack of education."

"I'm not talking about who your families are. I'm talking about who you and Jim are today. Your lifestyles are not compatible," he replied. I resisted this analysis. But when the professor confronted me with his opinion, I remembered a day when I came home from the grocery store with a car trunk packed with groceries. Jim helped me carry them in and put them away and then commented, "My stomach knots up just seeing what you are able to spend on groceries in contrast to how I am able to feed my two children when I have them."

I wanted to believe Jim and I could rise above this cultural definition of compatible lifestyles. I resented a neighbor suggesting I at least buy him a cheap but new car so "his junk heap wouldn't be parked in our neighborhood." I never resented paying for everything we did together. I do not know how it made Jim feel. My perception is that he accepted it as reality. I wanted to believe our love for each other would transcend all our differences.

A year after "The Big Break-Up," we followed through with the wedding. Six months into the marriage, we separated. We signed the divorce papers on what would have been our first anniversary; we went out to dinner to celebrate. I picked up the tab. Even after the divorce, we continued to date for a few more years, on again, off again. The final split came when I dated someone else, and Jim found his current wife. God bless them and enrich their marriage for years to come.

Jim, already an ordained Baptist minister when we married, continued to work on his Master of Divinity at Lexington Theological Seminary. He introduced me to this seminary, his greatest gift to me. I started by taking a class for my own spiritual enrichment. Though my professional speaking career was flourishing, I grew frustrated because I couldn't include a spiritual component in the corporate world. The spiritual hunger I sensed from my audiences during the early Nineties parallels the need today, perhaps caused this time by the recession. Jim challenged my spiritual and religious thinking and inspired me to get my Master of Divinity and listen for a call to ministry. The theological conversations, challenges and new perspectives returned my heart and mind to my little girl self who thought Southern Baptist missionary was the only role for her, but in a new and thoughtful way I never had envisioned. Though also Southern Baptist, Jim's family leaned on academics and brought the full force of the classics, Greek and biblical study to inform their faith. Our discussions over the radical equality Jesus professed, not only changed my faith, it informed my belief that people were not on a ladder, better and worse than the next person. This thinking also deluded me into deeming our own differences didn't matter in marriage.

A friend came up behind me at a dinner event when Jim and I were engaged and said, "You sure don't *look* like a minister's wife." I got back to her years later and said, "I guess you were right; I am not a minister's wife. I am the minister." Jim helped me see this.

Act Three

SCENE ONE

Defining My Faith

Sand is the water of the desert.
It can bear the traveler on its billows,
Or wash her cups
And clean her hands.
But when her body's
Racked with thirst
No counterfeit will serve,
And one would trade
One's kingdom in the sand
For one clear cup
Of sparkling, liquid water.
One faith is quite as good
As any other
Until the heart in thirst
Cries out for what is true.

— ROBERTA KELLS DORR, *Counterfeit*

Many people make no distinction between religion, faith and spirituality. In my life, these words represent progressive stages in the development of my spirituality. Religion connotes for me the baggage of childhood but also the weight of centuries and institutions, structure and divisive doctrine we humans lean on as we argue about God. Faith, the second stage of my spiritual formation, meant *acceptance* of what I had not *experienced* for myself. While this stage presents problems for some folks because by its very nature you accept rather than know, I rested well in this stage for many decades.

I now wiggle, squirm, resist and rest at the point in my journey I call spirituality. I have not reached a destination; I hope I never do. Spirituality is unknowable, and I want to always be searching and learning. When I experience a place of comfort and peace, I now call this place my spiritual center. By spiritual center, I mean the source of all that's good and virtuous about human beings; some may choose to call this quality or essence our God-source, God, Higher Being. Pastors are currently railing in pulpits all across our nation about the spiritual-but-not-religious (SBNR) crowd. While I understand some of their angst — after all their job is to fill the pews and perpetuate the institution of the church — I also object to writing this group of spiritualists off with a broad swipe. But then, I'm the rare SBNR who attends and believes membership in a body of diverse believers is part of my spiritual life. Community is essential to my belief. We meet God and come to our spiritual center in many ways, one of which is when we draw near to each other.

So what are my routes to this spiritual center?

In 2006, my husband, John, and I packed up for the trip back to Camp LeJuene to return 15-month-old grandson, Tristan, to his parents. Tristan, a Charlie Brown look-alike, sat snuggly in his car seat sporting his custom-made Charlie Brown t-shirt. Spratley, our chocolate lab/border collie, normally a back seat pacer sat trapped in the space left to her by Tristan's car seat. As the miles cruised by, John and I lifted our voices in song with the St. Olaf College Choir CD (John sang in this choir of all choirs as a student). At first with subtlety and then with confidence, we heard Spratley crooning along — not barking, crooning. Then I turned to watch and realized Tristan had joined us too with his delicate little sound blending with the rest of us in a celestial quartet. Our car transformed into the world's smallest cathedral, drowning out the noise of the interstate, as these non-verbal creatures sang with passion and abundant joy. As with all transcendent moments, the essence defies adequate description, but I know I will never forget the experience: I heard the voice of God.

I also hear the voice of God through my choice of reading materials. God did not stop speaking when the Hebrew Scripture, the New Testament and the Koran were finished. Even some novels guide me down the path to my spiritual center, most notably *A Prayer for Owen Meany* by John Irving and *The Secret Life of Bees* by Sue Monk Kidd. Anne Lamott, Wally Lamb and Barbara Kingsolver have all guided me spiritually. In addition to fiction, I find the great thinkers of any age can assist in the development of our spirituality. Daniel Pink's *A Whole New Mind,* decidedly *not* a religious book, challenged my spiritual thinking with his concepts about right brain/left brain and my role in the world as a right brain person. Pink also pointed me toward Andrew Delbanco and his great history of spirituality in America, *The Real American Dream: A Meditation on Hope.* Delbanco says, "The most striking feature of contemporary culture is the unslaked craving for transcendence." I agree and find I am compelled to search for this transcendence in multiple ways.

Nature, on most persons' pathways to spirituality, eludes me much of the time because I'm too focused on what critter or bug might approach. We don't need a psychiatrist to diagnose my insect phobia roots down in the shabby houses of childhood where all manner of bugs lived alongside us. I long to get to a place so many folks claim as spiritual communion with nature, but creepy crawly things, well, creep and crawl.

Another path to spirituality for me lies in relationships. Have you crossed the divide between human beings when you know that your souls have touched each other with thought, word, deed, art or emotion? I have. Such moments for me have created spiritual nirvana. In that moment, you move beyond the separateness of your own skin and experience a oneness of heart and soul with another. This peak spirituality has occurred for me when I have worshipped with others, laughed with family or friends, in intimate conversations, performing and listening to music and during sex with my beloved. I touched the soul of another as we each moved to our spiritual centers.

I learned lessons that guide me on this spiritual journey. In my childhood, I learned all persons must accept Jesus Christ as Lord and Savior or be condemned to hell. Even primitive people in the farthest reaches of foreign countries must be saved by Southern Baptist missionaries. What surprise and relief to discover that I did not have to conform to those beliefs and that I was not personally responsible for ensuring every person on the planet ascribed to my particular religion.

We speak the biggest truth about God when we teach children the simple phrase, "God is love." To give and receive love is the only thing about which we can be sure, *regardless of what we name the power of love.* If you can't name the experience of love — God, Higher Power, religion, faith, spirituality or mojo — claim the power of love anyway. If you can't believe in a father figure or even a mother figure who lives above your head, claim the power of love. If you can't believe in heaven or hell or afterlife of any kind, claim the power of love. Then *practice* the power of love. I believe the power of love allows us to give to others, forgive others, understand each other and, most notable of all, to be able to give, forgive and understand strangers and even enemies.

I love my church, which is part of the Christian Church (Disciples of Christ), not because it is perfect but in spite of its flaws. Anthony de Mello, SJ, in the dedication of his book *The Song of the Bird* speaks for my heart on this matter of organized religion.

> This book has been written for people of every persuasion, religious and nonreligious. I cannot, however, hide from my readers the fact that I am a priest of the Catholic Church. I have

wandered freely in mystical traditions that are not Christian and not religious and I have been profoundly influenced by them. It is to my Church, however, that I keep returning, for she is my spiritual home; and while I am acutely, sometimes embarrassingly, conscious of her limitations and narrowness, I also know that it is she who has formed me and made me what I am today.

I have been formed by Christianity.

With time and growth, I now believe spirituality serves me best when the spiritual matches my temperament, my cultural views in a very broad sense and my educational inclination. I can't be black, Jewish, Greek or a thousand other characteristics I'm not. So I must figure out what it means to be white, female, American, Christian, Southern and be in relationship with the God of my understanding. And, I must do my best to understand, embrace and love those who are different in any and all ways.

SCENE TWO

Building My Karass

The last thing one knows is what to put first.

— PASCAL

Kurt Vonnegut coined two neologisms that were very useful to me in my practice of psychotherapy: karass and grandfaloon. By grandfaloon he meant an essentially meaningless grouping. The example he gave was Hoosiers — people who just happened to reside in the state of Indiana. He defined a karass, to the contrary, as a truly meaningful group.

It was helpful to probably half of my patients when I explained that their families were grandfaloons. What a relief it was for them to discover that they were not necessarily obliged to like their parents or their siblings. Strangely, this discovery often made it easier for them to love these same relatives, to provide for them and care insofar as it was in their power to do.

— M. SCOTT PECK, *Abounding Grace*

What sweet irony that Vonnegut used Hoosiers, my family's Indiana *grandfaloon,* as an example. He could have chosen my family instead. This grandfaloon phenomenon in my life — family as meaningless group of people with whom I reside — forced me to create family elsewhere on my own. Church (but not all churches) created one-of-a-kind *karasses* for me, meaningful groups where identification extended beyond a formal group label. But mostly, individuals came into my life and I built a *karass* of my own, person by person.

169

Six months after my husband Bart died, one scary afternoon in 1986 the worst tornado ever to hit Lexington, leveled the home of Bazz and Rachel Childress. As rain came down in sheets and wind blew every item not tied down, they moved what remained of their entire lives into our garage and themselves into our home, which we soon dubbed The Bartella Motel. This new family created by catastrophe became the seedbed of two relationships that have enriched my life and taught me again and again about the connection between trust, honesty and security. I had known Bazz and Rachel through church choir and from a few occasions when they babysat Mark and Sims. I would not have said I knew them well.

Shortly before the tornado, Aunt BJ had asked to stay with me while she switched to a new job. She had moved into the lower level of our house. We now had four adults, five cars, two children, three cats and two dogs, hence, The Bartella Motel.

When claims agents declared Bazz and Rachel's house a total loss, they began to look for a new home. The house that stole their heart would not be finished for a few more months, so the Bartella Motel extended to meet the need. During these months, we stockpiled memories, happy times like salty popcorn and sweet milkshakes after Sunday night church meetings. We shared moments of unconditional love when tempers grew short and the challenges, funny and annoying, of misbehaving children and pets required understanding. Most remarkable, we experienced the creation of a family based on trust — profound trust that these folks would be truthful while still being loving, intimate and committed to our relationship.

We joked that the intellect and energy of all four adults were required to get Sims through sixth grade. We laughed when Aunt BJ, who worked third shift as a nurse, would come home in the wee hours of the morning and eat the lunches Bazz and Rachel had prepared for the next day. We learned a Labrador puppy can eat a whole can of Frito bean dip (*can* and all), Rachel's flip flops, my best Italian heels and a $580 check.

Our church friends chuckled at this strange family developing beyond friendship. Bazz and Rachel were both extreme introverts; I am wildly extroverted. Bazz, a phenomenal thinker, came from a drastically different political perspective than I do. Rachel would self-identify as a rule-follower if not a bit rule-bound. I lean far more toward principle and expediency than to rules.

Wrestling on the floor, chasing around the swimming pool and shooting pool in the basement, Bazz became a father-figure for Mark and Sims — a godsend in this critical time of loss and grief for the boys. Bazz continued in this relationship with them until his death in 2012. He taught them to roughhouse, to shoot guns (against my wishes) and to be men in ways I couldn't teach them. He provided a sounding board during turbulent years and knew way more than I did of their boyhood secrets.

A new concept started soaking into my psyche slowly like steady rain on dry land: relationships built on trust become family, whereas family relationships based on mistrust never become intimate.

A recent nightmare illustrated anew the role Rachel has played in my life. I must have been pondering the vast significance of a new charm bracelet while falling asleep. In my nightmare, I was aware the charm bracelet provided a profound metaphor for my life. The charms, the kind which slide on a slim snake-like bracelet, were chosen to represent significant parts of my history. But the charms fell off the bracelet and rolled all over the room. I couldn't control them or find them or put them back together again. I felt distraught, out of control and panicked. Very disconcerting but not a surprising metaphor. The *next* night — I'm not making this up — I dreamed I was begging Rachel to fix the bracelet and to please, please make the charms stop falling off and scattering out

of my control. Of all the persons in my new cast of characters, I chose to entrust the task of holding my life together to Rachel.

I began to realize the by-product of relationships based on trust is space for both persons to thrive. While building trust requires time, patience, effort, love, patience, skill — did I say patience? — living honestly created freedom for me. Freedom comes through knowing that this person to whom I'm relating understands and trusts the worst of me and, thereby, grants me the space to be the best of me.

༄ ༄ ༄

We called her LaLa because that's how her name came out when son Mark began talking. She came to work for us in 1977, the year Mark was born. I was 30 years old and had zero experience with household help. I didn't even know other people who had household help. I certainly didn't know protocol applicable to white people having "colored help." Recently having read, *The Help* by Kathryn Stockett, I chuckled about similarities in the novel with how LaLa and I, over 25 years, broke down the rules and formed a friendship that continues today. Without doubt, she knew the rules and mores of white people having black "help" which I didn't, and probably wanted to teach them to me, so as to be more comfortable. But we forged a new brand of relationship instead.

The name LaLa stuck, but nothing else stayed the same. She arrived at work in her street clothes and changed into a white uniform. In the last years she worked for me, she still arrived in good clothes and changed, but she changed into her sweat pants and t-shirt so as not to soil her good clothes. If she ate at our house, she waited until I had gone out and then sat in the kitchen. This pattern crumbled with great resistance, but in the end, we could sit at the table and have a sandwich together and chat.

In the beginning, I knew little of her home life. In the end, I knew her family, knew her sorrows and knew her joys. I attended her family weddings and funerals. She could ask me to take her to the hospital for a test because all her family was working. We laughed over her family's foibles and strengths like we did over mine. She loved reminding me her husband, Warren, could "do anything except make money." She lovingly reminds me when I share the latest news of Sims, "Miz B, Sim-bones has been his own man since he was a little boy." We *knew* each other's families.

During the early years, LaLa also worked for the Shraders across the street. Because Mark and Sims saw her there when she was not at our house, they thought she lived there and that Mrs. Shrader was her mother. As children, they did not see black and white skin color as a deterrent to being family. We still don't.

Through four of my husbands, LaLa held her tongue and her opinions about men and dating. I wish she had not.

One morning when she arrived for work, I flew into her arms and sobbed. The realization Bart was going to die had just hit me. LaLa consoled and listened, then went about her work — one of many times we would cry over what life dishes out. She did, however, pout about the hat I chose to wear at Bart's funeral. I refused to be solemn and wanted to think of the service as a celebration of his life. The vivid purple suit and gray hat with the veil struck the right chord in my mind. LaLa mumbled for days about my outfit being inappropriate. After his death, she started bringing me a second cup of coffee as I put my makeup on each morning because that's what Bart used to do.

LaLa attended three of my weddings, and we have shared more funerals than we care to count. I know the small African-American church in her little town of Keene and have been welcomed there as family for her husband's funeral and her granddaughter's wedding.

As I moved through six residences, LaLa moved with me. She even continued to care for us during the short time I lived in my fourth husband house, smaller than her own home. LaLa and I both enjoyed the years when I lived alone in my small condo in downtown Lexington. She loved hearing the news of friends and seminary experiences and enjoyed meeting the guys I dated. Sometimes she would roll her eyes without saying a word.

Miss Celia, the poor white trash character in *The Help,* comes closest to who I was when LaLa and I first met. While college educated and, hopefully, possessing better taste than Miss Celia, I had more in common with "the help" than with the ladies in my women's club. And LaLa surely had more knowledge about managing a home, entertaining guests and being middle class than I did. She taught me gently about laundry and polishing silver, and despaired that I seemed incapable of organizing a kitchen.

Over the years, she checked my outfit before I went out the door and became more than comfortable expressing her opinion. She cared for my clothes in loving ways, even washing my stockings by hand. I know my way around an iron and ironing board, but my skills were no match for the artful ironing LaLa gave to a man's shirt or to my most delicate silk blouse. On a couple of occasions, however, she put a dollar bill on the counter and said, "Miz B, take that shirt to the cleaners. It's too hard to iron." I took the shirt and left the dollar bill. She still calls me Miz B even though I am now officially Miz P. When she called to tell me her husband had died, she used my given name — the first and only time. Our relationship transcended the tradition, but her ties to certain cultural norms stood fast.

On the anniversary of her 20th year of working for us, Mark and I created a money tree commemorating our time together and giving her a bonus. The three of us cried together over the shared memories like

the time during our early years when the clothes dryer caught on fire when drying a heavy rug. The episode pushed LaLa to tears for fear we would expect her to pay for the dryer. We also laughed over the period in which we called ourselves The Poop Ladies because Mark's diapers had to be changed constantly due to his lactose intolerance. When my lesbian stepdaughter and her partner came to stay for two months, LaLa adjusted and called them "Those Girls" but never once implied judgment.

LaLa's call on each anniversary of Mark's death is one I can always count on. She grieves the loss along with me. Mark would come in the door and yell, "LaLa, give me some sugar" and throw his arms around her. She always called him Mark Robert and called Sims, Sim-bones. She spoiled them by cleaning their rooms when I asked her not to do so, but she loved them and contributed to the color-blindness we taught in our home. LaLa has been an essential member of my *karass* for 37 years.

⋐⋑ ⋐⋑ ⋐⋑

Of course, Leah and her partner, Cynthia, remained essential members of my *karass*. In 1996, when Cynthia discovered she had breast cancer, I flew to Philly to stay with her overnight at the hospital so we could conserve Leah's energy and time for the recovery period. Then in 2002, the news came that Cynthia's cancer had returned. She lost the battle in 2007. We cherish the richness she brought to our lives with her music, her loving demeanor and her original perspective on life.

With the deaths chipping away at our *karass*, Leah and I now cling to each other and value this unique relationship between two persons who could not be more different on the surface, yet share a depth of values and honesty as rich as any seam of gold.

To say my family of origin never added to my *karass* would be inaccurate. But they have come and gone and their contributions to the

structure always proved wobbly. My husband, John, jokes that I need to stay off the Internet before I find more relatives. Through Facebook, I found one of my brother Bill's sons. He moved to the Northwest — about as far as he could get from his dad in Florida — and took his mother's maiden name because he didn't want to share the name Sims with his alcoholic father. Bill's sobriety and Chris' independent life allowed for some rebuilding of the bridge before Bill died.

I broke a promise to my second husband, Bart, that I would not help my family financially when I helped my sister Margaret on several occasions. But when sister Vivian called me from a homeless shelter, I refused to take her in because I knew she needed to figure out on her own how to clean up the mess that was her life. People would say one of those decisions was good and one was bad. But there would be wise people who chose different answers.

My sister Ashley wrote to me in the Nineties to thank me for how I raised her when Mom couldn't or wouldn't. But she hosts "family reunions" which I'm not invited to because I'm not part of that *Karass,* I don't think it's a *grandfaloon* because the group has great meaning for them. I'm just not part of it. I agonize over whether I could have done more to help even one of my sisters finish college, make fewer bad choices or experience fewer traumatic events in their crossing into adulthood. Or could I have done something that would have made at least some of us a *karass* instead of a *grandfaloon*?

めて めて めて

When I issued an invitation to the congregation for those interested in being part of a small group to encourage their spiritual growth, 15 persons showed up — all women. We divided into two groups, roughly along age lines.

179

When the younger group met, we named ourselves Kindred Spirits. Even as their pastor, I expected little beyond the once-a-month meeting, a study of spiritual materials and pooled thoughts about our faith experiences. Oh, ye, of low expectations. In the following 14 years, we have fed each other's souls. We didn't know about well-recognized research on conversation with sisters making for a happier life, and we didn't need for the sisters to be biological. We lived it out.

From the beginning, in 1999, we fused intense spiritual work with serious fun. One of our first outings together, we dressed up and set out for a day of thoroughbred racing at Keeneland Race Track. Seated in a box, laughing, chattering and soaking up the spring sunshine, we attracted the attention of a guy in the box next to us. Men seem to find it hard to resist the female energy of women enjoying each other.

"What kind of group are you all?" he asked.

"We are a spiritual life group from our church," Mary replied.

His eyes grew wider, and just as I pulled my shoulders back to take my jacket off naturally exaggerating my bust, Mary added, "And this is our pastor."

His mouth couldn't work fast enough, "What kind of church is that?"

Rosemary, our resident comic and wit, didn't miss a beat in replying "The Church of What's Happenin' Now."

We collapsed in laughter.

Perhaps, we would not have chosen each other as friends had we met under other circumstances. But life tossed out experiences that could have bonded us to each other or driven us apart: two graduations, five marriages, one divorce, two babies, seven grandchildren and more deaths than any small band should have to bear. Tears and sorrows demanded that we share them; their weight too much to be borne alone. We've nattered through romantic breakups too numerous to count and tended each other through more surgeries than we acknowledge — the flotsam and jetsam of six lives inextricably woven together.

Three biological sisters — Rhonda, Lisa and Martha — predisposed the circle toward blood-like commitment. Rosemary, a Maryland transplant, sought a local substitute for her own remote family. And Mary's years of broken relationships steeled her determination to "keep it real." We hailed from four different decades, 20s to 50s, in the beginning, Martha was still in college.

The diversity of this group provided a richness which comes from being friends with people who have walked very different journeys — economically, socially, educationally. Two of us have masters degrees; one has a high school education. Our salaries range from minimum wage to six figures annually. Our differences, which became our strength, taught me to be myself and I would not feel isolated or responsible, I could just be me.

I spent so much of my life trying to find a place in society where I fit comfortably. I wish I had known earlier how much diversity is key to making everyone at ease. I didn't have to be in charge of the world to feel secure, I could just bring my unique skills to the table.

When we first formed, Mary, a many-years-sober alcoholic, redheaded triathlete, influenced us to select for our first study material, *The Twelve Steps: A Spiritual Journey,* a book modeled on AA's Twelve Steps. This nitty-gritty guide necessitated that we dig deep and disclose courageously. So we did. We started by telling our life stories with truth and trust. I recommended this step for a group setting off on a spiritual voyage together. And I advised that we hold ourselves accountable to each other.

What made these friendships work? Trust, accountability and a fierce commitment of time. Teaching each other to live authentically required all three and more. We have studied self-esteem, shame, sacredness and relationship to God, other and the world. Trust has been the key to growth. If we had not felt secure in the ability to trust one another, we would not have accepted being accountable. I don't want someone knowing the most vulnerable parts of me, such as being sexually abused, if I can't trust them. I don't want someone challenging me to deal with that part of my life if I don't trust them. Trust means safety. Safety means being able to ask the hard questions, make the hard statements.

"That's not your problem. Give it back to your husband; it belongs to him."

"What are you doing to care for your health this month? Girl Scout Thin Mints do not count as a healthy choice."

"Is this guy you're dating enriching your life or an avoidance of something else?"

"Didn't we commit to a full day of retreat? Why are you saying you need to go back to work? Home? Shopping? Are all calendars clear for the third full week in July next summer?"

Building the bond didn't mean the conversation had to be heavy and directive. The dailyness of living also provided glue: a new dress bargain Mary found, Lisa's latest iPhone app, Martha's stories about her growing daughters, the antics of Rhonda's dogs and, of course, Rosemary and me bragging about grandchildren. The nothing-talk created the comfort of connection while the challenging material and fierce authenticity spawned our growth individually and collectively.

On more than one occasion, our raucous laughter caused onlookers to ask, "What can possibly be that funny?" Perhaps they missed Rosemary's suggestion that we raise money for the church by producing a calendar of me draped over her husband's antique Corvette. Rose alone could have kept us laughing through the years. Surely, those spectators failed to notice when Lisa's magnetic bracelet picked up her spoon from the elegant white table cloth at the restaurant. We guffawed while trying to retain our sophistication.

This flock has enriched my life in multiple ways. Mary has taught me how to deal with alcoholics in my past, present and future. Rhonda has modeled a stunning example of steadfastness and introversion, often absent in my own life. Lisa has shared her love of style and even shopped for the shoes to match the yellow silk suit I wore to my son's funeral. Rosemary physically held me upright the day I resigned as their pastor after my son's death. And Martha introduced me to my soulmate and husband, John.

These women have not shied away from telling me what I have given to them. The list included the ridiculous and the sublime. Rhonda said I taught her and her sisters not to wear horizontal stripes because of their broad shoulders. She also maintained that I gave her permission to question all things sacred so as to deepen her spirituality. As pastors, passing along what we learn in life is as important as passing along what we learned in seminary.

Martha, the youngest of our group, has shared in these 14 years her graduation from college, marriage and birth of her children. She has grown from a college girl into a multitasking business professional, wife and mother. At one point, Martha told me "You are a mentor and guide for all areas of my life. Period."

Rosemary, the artist among us, reminded me that I gave her a book about using the visual arts in worship, which freed her to worship in a way that reached her soul as nothing else had. She also said I gave her permission to be an imperfect Christian and not beat up on herself about sin. Her sleepless nights as a teen and young adult were spent worrying she would burn in hell for sins she has learned have nothing to do with God's love for her, and are probably not worthy of the word sin.

I would not have been capable of these rich relationships earlier in my life. Age has helped. Therapy has helped. The crises this group has

lived through with me demanded a new level of vulnerability than I had ever been willing to show.

My nomadic childhood and the challenges dished out to me necessitated that I learn on my own how to do relationships. I know this much is true — when I die, my list of honorary pallbearers will be the girlfriends who have carried me in life. In addition to the Kindred Spirits, there will be Linda, Rachel, Wendy, Vonda and Boog.

✢ ✢ ✢

"Don, this is Brenda. I can't go on. I can't live with the intensity of this grief. I don't know how you and Vonda have done this, but I can't. Please tell me what to do."

I knew with certainty the Lichtenfelts were the right persons to call when I didn't see a way forward with the weight of overpowering grief. The tragic bond between parents who have lost a child spins between even strangers like a microscopic spider web but with the strength of iron.

"Brenda, where are you?" Don asked.

"In my car."

"Please go home or come to our house immediately." Don said.

I don't remember the arrangements, but my emotional memory lives on with clarity that the Lichtenfelts were soon by my side and have never left me alone on this journey of grief.

Some people come into our lives for a season, for a decade or even for a brief encounter; others come in to our lives forever. I don't know why this is the case, but I have experienced the truth of it.

The Lichtenfelts came in to my life for eternity. I know this as sure as I know my own name. We met when we joined Central Christian Church in Lexington at the same time. A newcomers group oriented us about Central, but Don's 40 years in ministry taught him that new members needed to find their place in a church and old friendships are sometimes hard to break into. So we started a group of our own to meet, eat, and with luck, grow spiritually from our collective experience.

The group came and went; my deep friendship with the Lichtenfelts held firm. From the evening they first met John to bestow their stamp of approval or withhold it, John completed our tight foursome: folks who know each other so well we can hit each others soft spots with a pea-shooter at six feet or make each other laugh until food comes out our nose or we pee in our pants, whichever comes first.

During our years away from Lexington, the Lichtenfelt homestead became our favorite bed and breakfast. Coffee in our pajamas on the screened-in porch overlooking Don's wondrous garden has created spiritual moments for me that continue to inform who I am. Okay, maybe, I was the only one in pajamas, but sleepwear and no makeup for me verify the vulnerability I am willing to expose to Don and Vonda.

In spite of, or because of, Vonda's countless lectures to Don, he remains incapable of conversing with me without "zinging" me. Never once have these zingers made me doubt his love for me. And, sadly for Don, his zingers have also failed to improve my behavior or my spicy language. My best comeback to him came when a customer viewed a portrait of Don that hung in John's photography studio.

"Is he a model?" she inquired.

"Oh, no," I quickly informed her, "Don is not a model of anything."

Forever since, Don signs his name as "Not a Model." How *apropos*. I had to throw that last sentence in because Don hates for me to use foreign words.

Vonda, the planet's most extraordinary hostess, continues to look like Miss America in her eighth decade with style and grace. Behind her lovely exterior hides the Iron Maiden. Life has tossed the Lichtenfelts more than their share of tragedies; Vonda models for all of us how adversity doesn't have to define who you are. And, by the way, she has the cleanest house Good Housekeeping ever profiled. I'm sure her tombstone will say, "I found that last speck of dust, so I quit."

As we often have, one evening over dinner we started to become philosophical. Don questioned what he could possibly label a success in his life. Never mind, that he had 40 very successful years in ministry and is a successful husband and father by anyone's standards. On this night, he wanted to count success in the ways of the world: books published, awards won, positions attained, children who are presidents, etc. We bantered about the real definition of success, no shortage of opinions in this foursome.

And then I looked him in the eye, "Don, I am your success. I wouldn't be here today if it were not for you and Vonda. And I know undisputedly I am one among many."

ൟ ൟ ൟ

Linda Carruth Hager Davis and I met when we both drove the carpool from hell. How can four three-year-olds bring a fully functional adult to tears or send her back to bed each morning? It has been done and Linda and I are mothers to two of those children. Thus began a friendship of over 30 years and the addition of an essential member of my *karass*.

Though polar opposites theologically and politically, Linda and I can make each other laugh or sob in public. She is Lucille Ball-type funny, and I'm a receptive audience with stories of my own. At one of our hundreds of lunch dates, a gentleman from another table could not stop himself from stopping by to tell us "how beautiful two women are when they're having that much fun." Our contrasting approaches to life have

not kept us from sharing our love of clothes, makeup, music, theater, home decorating and especially our journeys with husbands and children. I always permit Linda to be president of Christians Who Cuss because as a conservative it's a bigger deal to her. I am perpetually vice president.

Linda and I have solved the problems of several marriages and five children, and if there is not world peace as a result of our lunches and walks, it is not for lack of trying. Most notably, during my yearlong marriage to Dan Moore, we walked on the hottest summer evenings and the iciest winter mornings to permit me to rant and rave and resolve this huge mistake I had made. As I have said, girlfriends get you through life. Linda and I have given each other thousands of dollars of therapy for the cost of a lunch.

Our journeys intersected in a powerful way in 2002 when Linda lay on my family room floor in her full length mink declaring she could not go on living. Her abusive marriage of 30 years had reached its nadir. John and I had just married in January, and Linda moved in with us in March. One night the repartee that the gentleman in the restaurant called "beautiful," caused John to drink straight out of the bottle of tequila at the dinner table.

Linda moved on to her apartment, her divorce and, eventually, her new marriage, which took place in our living room. I officiated for the ceremony, our dog Spratley was bridesmaid and John shot photographs. Linda and James now live in Homerville, Georgia, where James is a United Methodist pastor. Trips to Homerville always involve great laughter.

On our first visit to Homerville, James suggested we take a tour of the Okeefenokee Swamp. John jumped for joy with visions of his photographs dancing in his head. While touring swamps is not my thing, I thought: *How bad could it be just sitting in a tour boat looking at the flora and fauna.* Touring swamps would be even lower on Linda's list of things to do. But we agreed to be good sports for the love of our husbands.

We arrived at the swamp and purchased our tickets in the office-gift shop. They directed us toward the dock. I looked around for the tour boat, but the water seemed pretty shallow for a big tour boat. Then a woman who identified herself as our guide approached and directed us toward this *very* small metal boat with an outboard motor.

"This? This is our tour boat?" I exclaimed as my eyebrows arched into question marks.

"It's okay, Bren. Be a good sport," John prods as he and James step gingerly in to balance both ends of the boat.

"Come on," they both say at once holding their hands out to Linda and me.

We each obey our husbands as if forgetting we are strong-minded, independent women. The tour guide indicated her husband was busy today, but she was pleased to be leading us through the swamp. My confidence in her began to fade. As she tried to start the motor three times, my faith in her ability to return us to the dock jumped overboard. Finally, the motor roared into life, and we wobbled away from our safe mooring. We had moved a mere six feet when live alligators moved with experienced assurance toward both sides of our little boat! Real. Live. Alligators. With mouths open wide, big teeth visible to terrified tourists, the no-doubt hungry creatures saw a small, wobbly boat full of lunch — curb-side service. Linda and I started screaming and grasping at James and John. Linda started first with the tears.

As I gathered a bit of composure, I yelled over the sound of the motor, "Linda, when you said you wanted us to travel together, I thought you meant five star hotels!"

Wiping her tears and fighting to control her sobs, she shouted back, "I did!"

✌ ✌ ✌

Fate was not finished with the story of Linda's divorce and my role in it. I was doing religious-political work in Washington, D.C. in 2004 when a random conversation with a journalist led ultimately to an article in *The Nation*† about Linda's abusive husband, who was a George Bush appointee to the Advisory Committee for Reproductive Health Drugs. Fortunately, my dear friend chose sanity and summoned the courage to not only leave the marriage but tell her story.

Linda and I nurture our friendship across the miles, through the years, and with grace on both sides, have built a bridge over our theological and political differences with planks of respect, love and integrity.

My favorite characteristic of a *karass* is that you never stop adding when you meet people who belong in yours.

† http://www.thenation.com/article/dr-hagers-family-values

SCENE THREE

My Own Brute Strength

But it is a common condition of being poor white trash;
you are always afraid that the good things in your life
are temporary, that someone can take them away,
because you have no power beyond your own
brute strength to stop them.

— RICK BRAGG, *All Over but the Shouting*

I pounded the pavement looking for a job the summer of my first wedding, no doubt wearing a preppy, sorority girl outfit such as my pale blue Villager dress and popular Bass Weejuns. Stop after stop, office after office, frustrating and no results. I needed one very good job or two mediocre jobs and I needed them now. Transportation, always a challenge because I didn't drive and didn't have a car, made finding a job I could get to an additional challenge. One interviewer said, "We prefer not to hire you girls with silver spoons in your mouths. We find you don't make very good workers." Huh? What silver spoon? My efforts at dressing up my reality with cute clothes and a current hairstyle had worked — to my disadvantage in this case. When the searching was over, I settled on two jobs. I worked all day as a waitress at a downtown hotel and worked the evening shifts as cashier at a grocery store.

One night that summer, emergency vehicles pulled up in front of the rental house I shared with my family in Evansville. The personnel searched for a neighborhood address. Not familiar with the neighborhood, I yelled to my stepfather, "Herman, there are firemen out front who need help finding a house!"

Herman didn't just watch TV, he was obsessed with it. He did not respond to my calls.

"Herman, it's an emergency. Come now!"

Frustrated and angry at not getting his attention, I stood in front of the TV.

He flew into a rage, screaming and swinging at me. He beat me with his fists, wrenched my arms, threw me to the floor and screamed at me. Finally, I cowered under the kitchen table to get him to stop. My physical injuries were minor except for a blood clot in my leg; my emotional injuries caused me to resolve no one would ever hit me again.

The next week, I moved to Trenton, Michigan, to spend the rest of the summer with my soon-to-be husband. When I quit my grocery store gig to move away from my family, my boss noticed my bruises and said, "If I had known you better, I would have been more supportive. I thought you were a wealthy college girl making party money." Shallow assumptions he made based on appearance. This incident provided a lesson, I couldn't dress up the girl inside me and expect others to see through and know her. It would be the first of many occasions when I thought my polished veneer worked for me, but it was off-putting for others and a barrier to them knowing who I was. More decades passed before this lesson sunk in.

Nerd, missionary, glamour girl, performer, activist and minister — I have played each of these roles during a segment of my life. I drifted from one to the other, writing and rewriting the script trying to make one of these identities work comfortably for my whole life. Good acting has always required knowing your character. How ironic I could study a character in a play and understand who she was, yet struggled to determine who I was or which role I could allow which people to see.

Plato insisted "The soul knows who you are from the beginning." Little consolation for those of us who have to spend entire lives trying to figure out what our soul knows. Even my handwriting took decades to settle in to being the left-handed, backward slant characteristically mine. Growing up and even into young adulthood, I didn't even know what it meant to know one's self.

❧ ❧ ❧

I was dubbed the "shy Univac" in high school (Univac was one of the first iterations of a computer) and the call to Southern Baptist mission work claimed my life from about twelve to twenty-one years old. The performer entwined herself with the nerd and missionary during this period, and I nurtured her through music and theater. I'm sure I rationalized why a missionary-to-be majored in speech and theater and minored in music. Whatever justification I conjured at the time, I either don't recall or I'm too embarrassed by the absurdity of my rationale to remember. The performer in me remained a consistent ground note, whether singing, acting, modeling, professional speaking or even preaching, I felt at home on any stage. This identity fit regardless of context or environmental changes.

Next came my fun role as glamour girl that started when I married my second husband and continued for decades. Fun. Exciting. But still a role that I was playing. On one cruise vacation, I packed 11 formal gowns for a ten-day cruise. I donned the two-piece vivid red palazzo pants and wrap blouse to sing in the passenger talent show. Performing with the orchestra on the ship and winning the contest sent my adrenalin soaring for days. The teenage actress finally could bankroll playing dress-up for real. While still in the hospital after the birth of our son Mark, I slipped into a full-length pink peignoir set with marabou feathers around the neck. Hospitals are public spaces, and I needed to play my role. I rejected any thought of what impression this outfit made on others. I wanted to play dress up, so I did. On another occasion, I remember putting my hand out the car window to grab a parking pass and upon seeing the three-quarter length white leather glove and blue shadow fox coat (which is actually stark white), I couldn't help wondering, "Is that really my arm in those clothes?"

More years passed before I realized the extent to which I had to dress up the poor white trash girl for her to feel okay. And even more years before I learned that each of the roles I played was off-putting to some people and isolating me to some degree.

I felt driven to perfect myself in order to reject and overcome my wacky, dysfunctional, unstable circumstances. On numerous occasions, this artifice served me well. At other times, my drive to erase the ugliness in my life worked at cross purposes with my goals. Even my children pushed against the façade. In family therapy when they were teens, my sons teased me about striving for the perfect house, wearing fashionable clothes, being well read and well spoken — in other words, perfecting my image. Mark wanted our house messier and more lived in. They labeled me ridiculously perfectionistic because I never went to the grocery without makeup applied and hair coiffed. On one occasion when my half-brother Dennis visited, he permitted me to drive his new red Corvette to Randall's on Romany Road. More than a supermarket, Randall's centered our neighborhood, and it required the healthiest of self-esteem to go in there with no makeup on. So to pick up a few groceries in a Corvette, I donned a white, strapless terry cloth jumpsuit with a red cinch-belt, wrapped my hair up in a matching turban, grabbed my sunglasses and scurried off to shop for onions and carrots.

Okay, they were right. But would they have understood if they could have felt my embarrassment as a child when having the occasional friend over? Would the boys have been persuaded to get off my back had they known the slings and arrows lofted at my self-esteem all through child-hood? At the end of that particular therapy session, our therapist turned to the boys and said, "Knock it off, guys. Those urges have served your mother well, and you need to cut her some slack." Wow, I loved hearing my polish worked at some level.

John insists I'm the stereotypical powerful, beautiful and sexy woman who threatens others — women especially — because of these qualities, while my self-image still includes the little knock-kneed girl from the projects, her mouth covered in fever blisters. He also thinks of me as a prized skipping stone. Skipping stones must be smoothed down *just so* to hit the water and continue skipping onward, making their impact on the smooth surface over and over again. But the very best of the skipping rocks has a little nick left in the rounded edge for you to grip securely as you launch it. I think I have moved beyond my need to polish and polish again and can embrace the nick. One of the hardest and most necessary skills I've had to develop is the willingness to expose qualities other than the polished veneer. I first had to recognize how I treasured the times when my negative thoughts about someone else turned into compassion when that person revealed vulnerability. Exposing my nicks and flaws has resulted in others seeing me with softer eyes, almost 100 percent of the time.

During the period after my second husband's death when I hurt mightily, an acquaintance commented, "Your grief has rounded off some of your sharp edges." Being unaware at the time that I had sharp edges that needed rounding, I felt hurt by her remark. Only later could I realize that to some I appeared brash, too strong, too independent, too self-confident — the negative effect of my expertly coiffed and well-dressed exterior shell. The need to maintain my façade also took a toll on my creativity. A writing instructor and two voice teachers over the years commented that they saw me as contained or too controlled. Another realization slowly sinking in, when I was unsure of who I was, I had to be in control.

As Good As It Gets, a 1997 movie with Jack Nicholson and Helen Hunt, tells the story of two imperfect people who find the humanity in each other. Jack plays a jerk with severe obsessive-compulsive disorder. He eats lunch every day at a restaurant where he demands Helen be his waitress as he maintains the excessive rituals that assuage his OCD. His relentless need for her presence in his life leads him to help her critically ill son, and they form a quirky but caring relationship in the process. Toward the end of the film, he tries to visit her apartment but finds the disorder there more than his illness can tolerate, so he suggests a walk at 5 a.m. Though walking at that hour seems bizarre to Hunt's character, she agrees. As they stroll along, Jack avoids the cracks in the sidewalk and attempts to convince Hunt that if they walk for 15 more minutes the local bakery around the corner will open and they won't be weird people at all: "We'll just be two people who like warm rolls."

That line went straight to the heart of me and ignited an understanding about myself and my family I had not grasped. When I'm walking down the street, no one but me sees the timid little girl. No one but me sees the colorful characters and alcoholics hanging from my family tree. It forced me to acknowledge what separates unhealthy or dysfunctional folks who behave in bizarre ways from the so-called normal folks can be as narrow as 15 minutes and a stop at the bakery for warm rolls. I spent far too much of my life trying to find, define and perfect normal when our life's task is simply to find yourself. I've turned the corner and I happen to like warm rolls.

Self-knowledge has come to me with as much resistance as the last drop of Grandma's white Karo Syrup. I have built a true self through discovering who I was *not*. Sometimes I'm hard on myself about having a winding career path, thinking I could have achieved so much more had

I settled on one occupation early and stayed with it. Sometimes I'm very hard on myself about marital mistakes, thinking there's nobility in being married 30, 40, 50 years to the same person. I now rest comfortably with who I am because I figured life out the hard way. And then there are the regrets, few in number but significant. I regret I didn't breast feed my children; I regret I didn't live in a big city and work before marrying the first time; and I regret never having lived in Europe. Only one of those is undoable.

Some years ago, I admitted to myself, out loud and to others, that I am compelled to speak truth *as I know it* — crucial modifying phrase. In truth, pun intended, that's all any of us can do. I have lived an interesting life of tragedy, joy, discovery and hard-fought-for peace; I owe it to others to speak truth.

Finally I am able to celebrate my particular history and circumstances and honor my authentic self. The values honed in the trenches of life are serving me well. I'm finding my security comes with trust, accountability and commitment.

SCENE FOUR

Eight Days Can Change You Forever

It is by going down into the abyss that
we recover the treasures of life.

— JOSEPH CAMPBELL

Deep, unspeakable suffering may well be
called a baptism, a regeneration,
the initiation in to a new state.

— GEORGE ELIOT

After the conference dinner, John and I walked back to the Edison Hotel in New York City via Times Square. Neither of us had been in New York for a while and it was great fun to just walk among the crowd on a Saturday night. The Naked Cowboy in his tiny tighty-whiteys strummed away and we stopped to buy a t-shirt for Mark. I have no idea what that t-shirt said or what ever became of it.

When we walked in to our hotel room the phone was ringing. Strange, I thought. Everyone calls us on cell phones these days. My niece, Margaret's daughter, sounded anxious from the start. "Bren, Rebecca has been trying to get hold of you all evening. Call her immediately. Mark has had some sort of accident."

I didn't panic right away. I'm a glass-half-full person who thinks every problem has a solution. "Don't worry. I'll call Rebecca right now."

Rebecca's voice sounded twice as anxious. She was driving with a friend from Huntsville, Texas, where she and Mark were in school at

Sam Houston State University, to a hospital in Houston. A helicopter ambulance overhead was taking Mark.

"They wouldn't let me ride in the helicopter with him because I'm not related to him! We don't know anything except he fell off the back of an ATV and hit his head. I was right behind him on another ATV and I thought he was joking when he got up. You know how he can be. Then he got very angry, almost violent and we knew something was wrong. The emergency vehicles came and they decided he needed to be flown to Houston."

After exhausting all questions and answers I could come up with, Rebecca said through her tears, "I'm so sorry, Bren. I hope he's going to be okay."

"Don't worry, Beck. I'll get on the phone with the hospital now and stay in touch until they know something."

The next few hours stretched forth as the eternal nightmare no parent ever wants to experience. I finally reached the neurologist who had already done surgery on Mark. He said that Mark's brain was swelling and that they did surgery immediately to relieve pressure. He would give me no further prediction of how Mark was or would be and said he would be in touch as they knew more.

Scared but still telling myself Mark would be fine, I decided to call a neurosurgeon in Lexington whom I had dated in the Nineties. When I got him on the phone and described the situation, he said, "Get a flight and get to Texas as fast as you can. Yes, I would have agreed to the surgery to relieve pressure."

I made the call thinking he would give me reassurance, now my panic soared. John began working on his cell phone to get me a flight and a taxi to the airport while I returned calls to Rebecca and family to update them. I shook with fear and chills as I dialed each number. John wrapped me in blankets with one hand as he held his phone with the other.

The taxi drive through strange parts of New York City would have scared me on other nights. Now I had far greater fears. He deposited me safely at the airport. I took a sleeping pill on the plane to force myself to get some rest on the flight. Realization set in that I would need all the strength I could muster.

I arrived at the Houston airport about the same time as Rebecca's mother coming in from Lexington. A friend of Mark's from Sam Houston State picked both of us up and delivered us to Memorial Hermann Hospital. I didn't have a choice of hospitals and would not have known how to choose, but I learned later that Memorial Hermann is one of the nation's best and the place where U.S. Representative Gabrielle Giffords would rehabilitate in the coming years. No parent wants or deserves to spend eight days by their child's side, never knowing if that day will be his last, but the staff at this hospital made the experience as bearable as they were able.

We scrubbed up to enter the ICU. Only two or three of us could go in at a time. Being very familiar with ICU, I walked in knowing what to expect. And yet. This time my dear Mark was lying there with tubes coming out of every orifice of his body, his head wrapped in bandages and multiple machines attached to him. I swallowed back the hot spit and willed myself not to vomit. I resisted the urge to climb onto the bed with him like when he was small and comfort him in the ways I knew so well from 25 years of parenting him.

Others arrived hour by hour. Sims flew in from Oregon, Leah from Philly, college friends drove over from Hunstville, his best friend Patrick Wallace from Kentucky, and an elementary school friend and my step-grandson who both lived near Houston. My sisters Ashley and Margaret, Rebecca's sister Hunter Quinn. And, of course, my dear husband.

John had flown back to Lexington, performed necessary duties with work and house and got to Houston as soon as he could. We had just married in January, this was April. From the moment the phone call came in New York until this day, John has been my tower of strength. Who thinks they're signing up for death and grief and catastrophic change in their wife three months after they say, "I do?"

The neurosurgeon gathered everyone present around a big conference table outside of ICU. The surreal atmosphere hung heavy around us. The people around that table loved Mark unquestioningly. But as the doctor asked and then listened to each person weigh in about Mark's life and death, I fought the urge to scream, "No! No! Nobody gets to decide about Mark's quality of life and pulling some plug except ME! I gave him birth! He is bone of my bone, flesh of my flesh! Stop it!"

Some shred of humanity or pastoral identity choked those words back. I knew the doctor was allowing everyone to have their say for multiple reasons — I suppose most compassionately to aid in the grief that was ahead of each one of us. Still, I wanted to cling to my baby boy with every scrap of maternal instinct in my being — primal ferocity.

The beeps and blips of the machines attached to Mark became familiar to us. His heart pumped on, young, healthy. His brain activity declined. By Wednesday, my intuition knew the boy I gave birth to was gone. Mark was so identified with his intellect. He once told me the curse of being smart was that "no matter what I become, I cannot exceed anyone's expectations. If I'm president, my elementary school teachers will say, 'I'm not surprised. I knew Mark would be something great.'" All that potential gone forever.

Still, there was my son's body, a big, beautiful, healthy body. We could not layer waste upon waste by burying his healthy organs with him. I wanted every usable piece of his body redeemed, reused, giving life in someone else's body. Thus began days with hospital ethicists, doctors, chaplains and social workers. In order to donate Mark's organs, he had to come out of the induced coma to verify brain death. I was scared. What would that mean? Would he feel anything? Would he know anything? So many questions, such medical answers but this was not their next patient, this was my Mark!

Thursday, Friday and Saturday, we took our turns standing by Mark's bed saying our good-byes — long, surreal, mind-numbing, gut-wrenching good-byes. We stared at the brain monitor, numbers that determined when they could declare the end of my baby's life. Numbers! Leah and I were the only two in the unit at one point, and we both used that moment to sing Mark the songs we each sang to him as an infant and toddler. Mine was an adaptation of a Christmas song:

> Long ago, there was born in the city of Georgetown,
> A sweet little babe, called Mark-ie Bar-tell-a.
> Angels sang at his birth, Lullaby peace on earth.
> Angels sang at his birth, Lullaby peace on earth.

Each person's grief and loss seemed to bury me under another layer. How can anybody, even me, the strongest of the strong, go on with the weight of this grief?

John's resourcefulness never takes a vacation. He got the idea and cautiously presented it to me that we might want to save some of Mark's sperm.

"You never know what the future will present, Bren. Will Sims need to use that sperm? Will Rebecca one day want to have Mark's baby? You never know."

The cruel twist is that John knew the pain of multiple miscarriages from his previous marriage, and I was too numb to have ever thought of this step. The hospital officially said, "No, we do not perform that service." John was tenacious. He found a urology intern who was willing to harvest the sperm; he found a sperm bank listed in a free local paper and the potential for future grandbabies toddled off to the bank. In

MBR

MAY 7, 1977 ~ APRIL 28, 2002

WE ARE COMFORTED BY YOUR KIND EXPRESSION OF SYMPATHY AT THE LOSS OF OUR BELOVED MARK.

෴

WHEN HE SHALL DIE
TAKE HIM AND CUT HIM
OUT IN LITTLE STARS,
AND HE WILL MAKE THE
FACE OF HEAVEN SO FINE
THAT ALL THE WORLD
WILL BE IN LOVE WITH NIGHT,
AND PAY NO WORSHIP
TO THE GARISH SUN.
SHAKESPEARE
ROMEO AND JULIET III,II,21

206

2006, after the birth of Sims' son, Tristan and Rebecca's marriage to another, we made the decision to discard the sperm. I have never regretted that we saved that piece of Mark for four years. Even the cremation plans were complicated. The medical examiner asked John, "Do you mind if your loved one is cremated by an African-American crematory?"

"Of course not," John responded.

"Well, then, it will be a couple of thousand dollars cheaper."

Another item to add to my list of injustices to fight.

Sunday morning arrived and John and I were in a car with some folks who were taking us to church. Who were those people? What church were we going to? How did this come about? My cell phone rang. The hospital. "Mark's brain activity has declined, please come now."

Saying that last good-bye with Mark's heart still beating haunts me. The number by which experts make such calls about life and death mean nothing to a mother walking away from her son's beating heart. As we walked out of ICU for the last time, Sims and I turned to each other and grabbed hold. The agony on Sims' face etched deeply in to my brain. Mark, the younger brother, had become the older brother in recent years. Now Sims would live the rest of his life without those phone calls, without the UK basketball trash talk to each other, without sharing their marriages, their children and Christmases to come. The grieving began a new stage. And we had to think of organ donation (see page 271).

We returned to Lexington and started plans for Mark's service. I'm doing the tasks. I'm walking, talking and sometimes sleeping, but feel strangely numb and removed.

Then my son arrived in a box one day. Just like Amazon or Overstock.com, a package came in the mail. I signed for it; accepted it into my hands and stood there unknowing. What is the next step when I'm standing there holding my son in a box?

SCENE FIVE

Grief, I Thought I Knew You

Time does not bring relief; you all have lied
Who told me time would ease me of my pain!
I miss him in the weeping of the rain;
I want him at the shrinking of the tide;
The old snows melt from every mountain-side,
And last year's leaves are smoke in every lane;
But last year's bitter loving must remain
Heaped on my heart, and my old thoughts abide.
There are a hundred places where I fear
To go, — so with his memory they brim.
And entering with relief some quiet place
Where never fell his foot or shone his face
I say, "There is no memory of him here!"
And so stand stricken, so remembering him.

— EDNA ST. VINCENT MILLAY

SEPARATION

Your absence has gone through me
Like thread through a needle.
Everything I do is stitched with its color.

— W. S. MERWIN

Grief seminars were part of my repertoire as a professional speaker. Having buried two husbands, my mom, my Aunt BJ and a close friend, I thought I knew a thing or two about the heartache of loss. No doubt the seminars were helpful to some listeners. The world, however, had far

more to teach me about sorrow. This new grief — gut-wrenching, life-changing grief — the physical, emotional and spiritual pain of losing my child stands apart from all other grief.

Though years since Mark's death, memories of what we shared continue to sneak up on me and trigger the grief of losing him. In 2004, I walked the campus of George Washington University and passed the law school where he almost chose to go because of the great scholarship they offered him. This drive-by shot of grief was based on the dream that he could have been there as a student when careers unexpectedly moved John and me to Washington, D.C. Mark would have loved the conversation and debate over my religious-political work with the Democratic National Committee and the Kerry/Edwards Campaign. He would have been right smack in the middle, arguing both sides about whether religious folks should start a political action committee. He would have pushed me to my limits obsessing over the fine points of controversy. It would have been great fun.

Another emotional sneak attack occurred when I was staring at *The Washington Post* rather than reading. *The Today Show* played in the background because my husband John can multitask on computer, newspaper and TV to absorb his morning media digest. The first chords of *Bad to the Bone* by George Thorogood broke through my morning fog, the soundtrack for Matt Lauer in a segment about riding a Harley on the open road. It was also the soundtrack for Mark's funeral service. As teens, when Mark and his buddies discussed plans for their memorial services, Mark proclaimed he wanted *Bad to the Bone* played at his. The ministers and I agreed blasting Mark's opus from the sound system in the holy sanctuary of Central Christian Church seemed a fitting tribute to his raucous sense of humor and Gen X spirituality. So we did. Hope it turned out to be all he intended.

Rebecca and Mark were high school sweethearts. If asked whether adolescents can truly be in love, I would say "not likely," the exception being Mark and Rebecca. I often told Mark, "If I had searched the world over and had the right to select, I could not have chosen a better woman for you than Rebecca." Some folks would even say Rebecca was Mark's salvation when after high school he fell into a do-nothingness that involved tending bar and smoking too much pot. I say Rebecca's love for and belief in Mark carried him when he didn't believe in himself. While she was experiencing a typical college life, she never wavered in her commitment to Mark. The three of us lived within a few blocks of each other during that period. Rebecca would sometimes come over to my condo to cry and complain that Mark wouldn't or couldn't grow up. But she saw the vast potential and believed he would push through, conquer the demons and realize his promise. When he reminded her that she had said they could get married when she graduated from college, she responded, "I thought you would be more mature by then!" So Mark agreed to get his undergraduate degree while Rebecca worked on her Master's.

In the last months of his life, Mark was deciding where to go to law school. John asked him, "Mark, why, if you have scholarship offers from some of the best law schools in the nation, would you want to stay here and go to the University of Kentucky."

He answered with one word, "Rebecca."

Watching Rebecca walk the journey of grief over Mark's death added to my own. I knew she might be hurting as much as I was, feeling the intense loneliness and isolation grief causes. I loved Rebecca not because Mark loved her but for who she was and continues to be. I was able to say to Rebecca after Mark's death that I didn't expect her to make being Mark's fiancé her permanent identity. I wanted a life-enriching future for her, and I hoped to one day dance at her wedding with the groom of her destiny. I underestimated the insidious shelf life of my grief. When the time came to dance, I could not even attend. Even the pictures seemed like they could have been of Mark and Rebecca's wedding with all their friends but with a stand-in groom. The pearl of this story though is Rebecca's groom is a charming, genuine fellow. Rebecca's cousin said at the time of Mark's death that his prayer for her is that she would find someone who would love her as much as Mark did. Fate delivered on that prayer.

I'm convinced, that in the weeks after his death, Mark watched with pride the way Rebecca conducted herself through the tragedy of his death. I'm convinced his heart swelled with love as she read a letter at two funeral services telling the world of the person she knew him to be.

I did not have the strength to speak about Mark at the time, and even in the years since, I find words inadequate to express my love for him. Nothing in my rich, challenging life defines me more than this grief; hence, my feeble attempt to express my love in a Letter to Mark.

Dear precious Mark Robert,

Words on a page cannot possibly convey the extent to which I miss you. The hollowness of your absence makes my throat ache, makes tears burn and makes my life without you not worth living.

Did I let you know in your short lifetime how extraordinary you were? How loved? How hysterically funny? How smart? How beautiful? How precious? How much *you* were the restitution for all else that was painful in my life?

So how do I grieve a relationship like ours?

In *The Year of Magical Thinking*, Joan Didion talks about "complicated grief" which gave me an explanation of why your death so devastated me — in ways all the other deaths I have endured have not. One situation in which complicated grief could

occur was grief in which the survivor and the deceased had been unusually dependent on one another. *"Was the bereaved actually very dependent upon the deceased person for pleasure, support, or esteem?"* (Italics mine)

As your generation would say, "Duh!"

When your Dad died and your brother started on his personal journey of misbehavior and self-destruction, you and I turned to each other and grabbed hold with everything in us. As the years went by and we both went on to other relationships, other pursuits, other cities, other growth, *we never lost that grasp.* That's why it hurts so badly. That's why it's "complicated grief," which I prefer to the term "pathological bereavement." There's enough about me that's pathological without adding another. Naming the grief does not help when I am sabotaged by memories: good times, bad times and all the in between times in the twenty-five short years of mothering you.

Is it my genetic code that makes everything high drama for me? Am I more sensitive to what has happened in my life than the average bear? Maybe, but many would say I'm stronger than the average bear in handling it. In fact, you said, "If a nuclear bomb went off in the back yard, Mom, you would be the only survivor."

Little did you know that *you* would be the nuclear bomb.

Love,

Mom

Anger accompanies grief. Anger at what? God, no. Mark, no. Life, yes. How can I stop grieving the loss of what constituted one of the richest elements of my existence? A therapist reminds me that as rich as it felt, my relationship with Mark was not the sum total of my life. True enough.

And I don't want my grief over Mark to shortchange my relationship with Sims and his treasured family.

In the months after Mark's death, I asked myself, "Why must the depression hang around so long and be so heavy on my heart and soul and mind?" Not that I had answers, but I asked anyway. Was it a protective armor, protecting me from the depths of grief into which I could actually fall and not be able to pull myself out? Some folks thought if I broke my unresolved grief into tiny pieces I would find peace ultimately and "cure" the depression. Damn hard work! If I don't do the grief work will there always be a part of me divided from the whole of me? What does wholeness look like? And, oh by the way, I'm fucking tired of working toward wholeness. Being born to Violet and Clarence gave me enough brokenness for one person. I want not to feel like a hollow shell.

A friend of mine suggested I heed Martin Luther King Jr.'s admonition to turn my grief into creativity. I replied to her, "On my good days, my writing and speaking is the creativity from my grief. On my bad days, I would say, 'screw you, Martin.'" And I would say to my friend who loves me and wants to move me down the road to recovery, "Get back to me when you have buried one of your sons."

Mark's death created a turning point. This bend in the road continues to lead me down new paths of discovery about what matters in life. I have always had more than my share of chutzpah, but Mark's death created even greater fearlessness. I have experienced the worst life can dish out and, therefore, I can be relatively fearless in moving forward.

In a departmental meeting of a non-profit for which I worked, our task was to bombard each person around the table with positive messages. When my turn came to receive the deluge, our departmental administrative assistant spoke first.

She hesitated, then said, "I don't know how else to say this: you have the biggest balls I have ever seen on a man or woman!"

As the folks around the table guffawed, I digested the "compliment" and decided the remark was, indeed, a compliment. "Why thank you. That may be the nicest thing anyone has ever said to me."

Although I didn't want the chance to prove my mettle, I discovered also that Mark's death has helped free me from attachment to money and things. As the recession of 2009 has given most of us a chance to grapple with that issue, I find in the face of burying my child, no possessions and no amount of money claim my loyalty or passion.

I am moved by the story of Kisa Gotami from an ancient Buddhist text.

Kisa's only son died. In her grief she carried her dead child to all her neighbors, asking them for medicine.

"She's lost her senses," neighbors said. "The boy is dead."

Finally, Kisa met a man who said, "I cannot give you medicine for your son, but I know a physician who can."

Kisa pleaded, "Please, please tell me, who is it?"

"Go to Sakyamuni, the Buddha."

Kisa went to the Buddha and cried, "Lord and Master, give me the medicine that will cure my boy."

Buddha replied, "I want a handful of mustard-seed and it must come from a house where no one has lost a child, husband, parent, or friend."

Kisa went from house to house and begged.

"Here is mustard-seed; take it!"

But when she asked, "Did a son or daughter, a father or mother, die in your family?"

"Yes, we have lost loved ones too."

Kisa found not one house untouched by sorrow and grief. Discouraged, she sat down and pondered, "How selfish I am in

this grief! Death is common to all but I know a path that leads
to immortality if we just surrender our selfishness."

Kisa buried her son in the forest, returned to the Buddha,
took refuge in him and found comfort in the Dharma which is
a balm that soothes all the pains of our troubled hearts.

I don't agree there is "a balm that soothes all the pains of our troubled
hearts." Some pain cuts so deep no balm can mend the wound. Oh, the
wound may come together and leave a scar rather than a gaping hole,
but a touch on the scar always renews the pain. I do believe, however,
that we find the sacred in the grief journey and on the way find those
who are walking the path also. This companionship of sufferers makes
the burden bearable. Sorrow will come to all of us; how we bear each
other's burdens tells the beginning, middle and end of the story. The
friends who have borne my grief by remembering Mark along with me
lift my spirits. Acquaintances who are uncomfortable with sorrow or
maybe afraid my grief will sully their polished exterior or bring tragedy
into their own life have left me alone in the valley. And the end of the
story is told by those who acknowledge I am this broken but authentic
grieving mother and accept me as that.

I embrace Elizabeth Kubler-Ross' simile of people being like stained-
glass windows. "They sparkle and shine when the sun is out, but when
the darkness sets in, their true beauty is revealed only if there is a light
from within." For me, inner light sometimes took the form of those who
had also walked this journey.

I experience redemptive moments in the company of dear friends,
Don and Vonda Lichtenfelt, who have also buried their own son. Their
courage, faith and care for me personify God's grace and love for all
who suffer. I experience spiritual moments when I am able to minister
to others in the midst of their grief.

But as hard as I've worked in therapy and as much money as I've spent on it, I'm scarred by emotional gashes and mutilations of life. After Mark's death, the scars manifested in panic attacks that, for me, are like evil orgasms. Whereas an orgasm radiates pleasure through your neurological pathways, panic attacks radiate fear and almost pain through those same neurological pathways. Debilitating. Scary. Feeding-on-each-other. I resolved, *once again*, to deal with them via exercise, meditation and Al-Anon. I knew lack of trust — most basic trust that life would go on and that I would be able to handle whatever life dished out — lay at the bottom of my panic attacks.

Damaging betrayals at the hands of family members wrote the tragedies for me — my father's neglect and infidelity, my mother's inadequacies, my aunt's molestation of me — to recount a few. But Mark's death and Sims' subsequent deployment to Iraq packed big punches to the gut. How could I trust anything or anybody in the face of those life events?

Healing in the first year feels uncertain and strange, as if I'm confused by blurry highway signs or giving birth once again. I have to get used to grief as in getting used to the taste of Stilton cheese. I have to learn to like its discordant music, wear it like a new perfume I have chosen that comes across strong and strange when I first put it on. The process of grief. And it is a process.

With time I am returning to a new version of the person I was prior to Mark's death. Healing comes, slowly, but it comes. I remember Albert Camus' words, "There is no sun without shadow, and it is essential to know the night. In the depth of winter, I finally learned that within me there lay an invincible summer."

The bottom line of grief is this: If the relationship had not been so good, I wouldn't hurt so much. There is a Mark-shaped hole in my heart no surgical team can mend. Would I give up the richness of my relationship with Mark so as not to experience the pain of this wound? Not in any lifetime! I embrace the invincible summer within me every time I think of him.

SCENE SIX

Life after Life

If I were dead and buried and I heard your voice
beneath the sod, my heart of dust would still rejoice.

— FROM THE MOVIE *ROMAN HOLIDAY*

In a conversation in *Eat Pray Love*, Elizabeth whined to Richard, the now famous Texan, that a guy she thought her true soulmate broke her heart. Richard lectures her on what a real soulmate is.

> People think a soulmate is your perfect fit, and that's what everyone wants. But a true soulmate is a mirror, the person who shows you everything that's holding you back, the person who brings you to your own attention so you can change your life. A true soulmate is probably the most important person you'll ever meet, because they tear down your walls and smack you awake.

Marriage to John smacked me awake from Day One — awake to my negative behaviors and the lack of self-knowledge that held me back. I disagree with Richard on one part of his theory. He says to live with your soulmate forever inflicts too much pain. Perhaps true with some, but my soul match with John gets richer with time and he continues to hold up the mirror to enrich my view of myself. Hallelujah!

It began on a Friday evening, I had just finished writing my sermon. I sat around in day-old makeup with no plans for the rest of the evening

221

— life is exciting for fifty-something women in ministry. I decided to call the phone number in the email to confirm I would meet this "fix-up" date at the designated time and restaurant. I assumed I would get a voice mail since people with real lives go out on Friday evening, but he answered his phone.

"I just wanted to make sure you received my email confirming to-morrow night," I stammered.

"Yes. But, hey, I haven't eaten yet. Want to go get a bite to eat now?" he asked.

"I've already eaten, but I will have a glass of wine while you eat."

"Okay, let's meet at Suggins on Romany Road."

Knowing he was a Northerner, I blurted out, "Don't you Yankees pick your dates up?"

A bare 30 minutes later, I had thrown on some walking shorts and was letting my dog do his business when John Lynner Peterson drove up and got out of the car.

"Oh my god, you're gorgeous!"

How could I not fall in love with a man who delivers that opener? I later learned his expectation could not have been much lower. Fifty-something unmarried minister translated to him as overweight, hairy legs with a bit of hair on her upper lip, a few wild ones on her chin, no makeup, sensible shoes and a very no-nonsense hairstyle. He later apologized for his unflattering characterization of female clergy.

After dinner and ice cream, we sat on my deck and sipped tequila until two in the morning. I had never "sipped tequila" in my life. We both knew that first night that this pairing felt ordained, serendipitous, divinely inspired and meant to be — take your choice; color your own dream. When John walked through a hallway of my house where I had hung photos of my life in the arts, he said, "I've been looking for you." Our mutual love of a variety of the arts provides one of many lenses

through which we see each other. John's genuine recognition of me satisfies an identity hunger at my core.

The story of how I met John will give middle-aged single women hope that the right person exists for all of us. For most of his career, John worked at the intersection of religion and media. In 1998, John produced the Fiftieth Anniversary Party for the World Council of Churches in Zimbabwe at which Nelson Mandela spoke. Doug Smith, a young minister who assisted him on this event said, "John, if you ever move into doing work on the Web, call me." Within a few years, Vision Interfaith Satellite Network, in cooperation with Hallmark (now Odyssey networks.org), hired John to start a website called FaithandValues.com. John thought the job required a move from Chicago to the Manhattan headquarters. He then received news that they had chosen to locate this venture in Lexington because of a random conversation on an airplane. (Are you getting the picture here about coincidences?) John responded, "You're moving me *where*?" Familiar with Manhattan, he felt comfortable there. But Lexington? He had never countenanced living there.

As requested, John called Doug and hired him to assist in development of the website. Lexington didn't feel as strange to Doug since he had gone to seminary here and served Newtown Christian Church as student pastor. As the dominoes fell, Doug hired Martha Johnston for FaithandValues.com, a young woman who attended his youth group at that congregation and had since graduated from college.

John, Doug and Martha busied themselves with building a Web presence when one day a light bulb brightened above Martha's head. She called me on a Monday at that same Newtown Christian Church where I served as her pastor. "Brenda, you need to meet the vice president of our company." Gutsy for a twenty-something to call her 50-ish pastor and suggest a hook-up.

"I'm game," I replied. "I'm not dating anyone."

Thursday evening of the same week, my cell phone rang while I was out to dinner with my sister. Martha initiated the conversation, "Brenda, give me a pep talk. I know the timing is right because he's still here and the work day is over but I'm nervous. I feel like I'm asking him out myself and he's old enough to be my dad."

"Martha, get your ass into his office. I'm not getting any younger!" So she did.

John emailed me and we made arrangements to meet on Saturday evening.

Our 12-year-old marriage has survived life events that rival what marriages of 30 years experience. Every day when I make my gratitude list, John ranks number one. And most days, we ask each other, "Will you marry me today?"

Marriage to John is my favorite example of how the imperfect can be the best part of life. We say to each other "You're not perfect, but you're perfect for me." We embrace my grandmother's saying about some couples, "They only spoil one household!"

Incapable of this rich, rewarding marriage earlier in my life, I did not develop patience for many years. The ability to admit my own imperfections arrived even later. I can still be that control-prone, hard-driven achiever with a low tolerance for foibles in herself and others. The ability to forgive others for their shortcomings brought the blessing of self-acceptance. The ability to acknowledge myself in all my garbage and glory allowed me to grow into who God intended me to be.

I have needed a mirror held up all my life — we all do — but those of us who come from dysfunctional childhoods with a lack of parenting need the mirror even more so. The richness of marriage to John allows me to see how I try to control in order to feel safe. Dear friends gave me a needlepoint pillow which says, "I'm not bossy. I just have better ideas." Sometimes John holds the pillow up to signal I've overstepped my boundaries about control. We laugh and then I back off. Our marriage has also allowed me to see gifts I have to offer to the world that I might not have claimed on my own. On the other hand, I remind John that I am not one of his siblings or his abusive grandfather. The mirror I hold up to John shows he developed negative reactions to cope with his abusive childhood. Then we move on.

John recognizes me regardless of the role I play in a moment. He knows the polished public speaker and the little girl who still awakens scared because of a bad dream. He delights in escorting a well-dressed wife to social occasions but knows and loves the woman of Medicare status even without makeup. John's encouragement concerning my creative ventures ignited the embers I dared not fan on my own. When I chose to prioritize my grandparenting role as Mimi to Tristan and Payden, John grew into the complimentary role of Pappa, a stretch for one who had no children of his own. And he gave me space, support and a warm body to lean into when the role of grieving mother was the only one I could play.

The richness of marriage to John lights my life, lightens my burdens and shines a light for me to see into my own soul. We share art, music, faith and grandchildren in such a way that John touches a core inside of me I didn't know existed.

One evening when we were photographing a charity dance in Raleigh, North Carolina, a young African-American woman came back to the registration desk to ask me in her honeyed, slow Southern drawl, "Couldn't you just sop him up with a biscuit?" I could and I have.

SCENE SEVEN

My Past Is Never Past

In 2002, John insisted on meeting Dad to see who gave me life, so on our way to visit his family in Minnesota, we made a quick stop in Evansville.

Dad had not mended his ways or his shirt but there he sat at The American Café. I had last seen him five years earlier when he arrived for sister Margaret's fourth wedding with his daily buzz already going. On this day, he appeared sober. He faced the window so he watched as John and I emerged from our car. John parked near the edge of the gravel lot so our dog Spratley could pee and burn up some energy. I walked on into the café.

His eyes did not leave me as I walked through the door and toward his table. I wasn't sure he even recognized me. I finally said, "Do you recognize this face?"

"Wuhl, I'll be goddamned. Where did you come from?"

"We're traveling to Minnesota and John wanted to meet you so we stopped by."

Since Dad ate two meals a day at The American Café, they didn't seem to mind that their regular customer had guests arrive at closing time.

Dad's grizzled, scaly, skin sagged, but the Paul Newman eyes shined on through decades of boozing. "That-Clarence-Sims-shit-eatin'-grin" worked its magic in spite of no teeth. Yet no one needed to be told the infamous womanizer was petered-out.

"We stopped at your house. Nothing was locked up so we went

through and called for you. I wanted John to see the picture of you with cameos of all six wives. And I knew he would get a chuckle out of your refrigerator with the keg and the outside spigot. Your river's still rolling, How are you?"

"Hell, I'm okay, just old."

"Dad, did you know…" I started to ask as tears formed over my eyes.

"I know, hon."

And that was all we said about the death of my son.

I am finally able to admit that I loved him and also able to admit that he was incapable of loving me the way I needed him to — but he loved me none the less.

SCENE EIGHT

I Can Never Stop Being a Mother

Grown don't mean nothing to a mother. A child is a child.
They get bigger, older, but grown?
What's that suppose to mean?
In my heart it don't mean a thing.

— TONI MORRISON, FROM *BELOVED*

The banging on the door awakened John and me both at the same time. He headed downstairs as I swam up from the depths of sound sleep and then followed him. I stood frozen on the stairway when he opened the door. Police officers at your door at 3 A.M. never mean good news.

I clutched my white terry cloth robe tighter hoping to keep out the chill of fear and the sudden urge to vomit. John accepted the small piece of paper from one officer's hand as the other man said, "Mrs. Peterson needs to call her sister Margaret immediately."

Our cell phones had been turned off and we didn't have a landline at that time, so Margaret contacted the police for help. Without another word being spoken, I knew the emergency related to Sims. He had just returned from Afghanistan that past week so I knew at least the crisis was not in war. The sensations of panic felt, oh so, familiar.

John and I grabbed our cell phones and sat close together on the couch. His big Scandinavian bulk comforted me without words. He too knew the message related to Sims. I called my sister and John started calling Sims' and his wife's cell phones. When I reached Margaret, she said, "Bren, give the phone to John." Numbly, I did as I was told.

John listened and took notes. Sims was in a hospital in Knoxville. He had shot himself in the mouth with his own gun. She urged us to get there as quickly as possible, but she could tell us no more about his condition. Sims and his wife, Tiffany, had been on a get-away weekend in Gatlinburg when the incident occurred.

John and I made calls for the next few hours. We made necessary arrangements for leaving our photography studio, dog and home, not knowing when we would be able to return. I finally got Tiffany's mother on the phone and she had a few more details but not much. Sims was in stable condition, Tiffany was hysterical and Tiffany's parents were on their way to Knoxville. The time between the officers' knock on the door and our arrival at the University of Tennessee Hospital felt like eternity in slow motion.

This was the second time I had walked in to an intensive care unit to see a son. Tension twisted every nerve in my body. *What will I find? What will my gorgeous son look like after a bullet flew through the roof of his mouth and out his left temple?* I finally laid eyes on my son. The left side of his face, swollen, bandaged and bruised telegraphed the gravity of his circumstance and the path of the bullet. He held up both hands as if to block me from coming into his curtained section of ICU. Neither his hands, nor a tidal wave could have stopped me from seeing and loving my child at that moment. He spoke little; his resistance to me seeing him like that turned him inward.

"I'm here, Simmies. I will stay right here until you're okay."

A long 24 hours later, the physicians assured us he would live. Their comments about his recovery were less positive. The diagnosis, severe PTSD, meant little to us at first. Several days after our arrival, the plastic surgeon rebuilt his left eye socket and cheek bone with cadaver bones and titanium. "It's too soon to tell whether he will be blind in the left eye, have compromised vision in it or be just fine."

What kind of miracle just happened? My son put a gun in his mouth and pulled the trigger and it missed his brain by millimeters. If this doesn't tell him God still has a purpose for his life, what will?

Post traumatic stress disorder constituted the next mountain we had to climb with Sims. What we called shell shock in World War II, afflicts thousands who have returned from Iraq and Afghanistan. The treatment Sims has received has proven inadequate to the task of the severity of PTSD.

Tiffany found out she was pregnant two weeks after Sims attempted to take his life. Our Payden Elise Bartella arrived May 20, 2010. We had moved to Raleigh in 2005 thinking it was a good retirement city. After weighing all factors, the urge to be near Sims and his fragile family during this difficult time pulled strong on our hearts and John and I moved back to Lexington, KY in February 2011.

On Sims' first visit to our new home in Lexington, he arrived with his baseball cap on, his collar turned way up and his shoulders hunched forward as if to protect himself. He remained in this posture throughout the evening. We soon learned this would be the version of Sims we related to on most days. Glimpses of the "old Sims" sparked our hope on a few days. You would have to know his face well to be able to see the scar and gentle, dent of skin on his right eye and temple. Perhaps only a mother's eyes perceive the change. We didn't know how to help, and he was not allowing us close enough to help anyway.

I practiced daily this parenting an adult male from afar. I gathered the safe topics about which we could engage as if herding stray sheep into a fold of fencing. UK basketball, Tristan and Payden, his golf game. But his time in Iraq and Afghanistan, his brother's death, his relationship with me — all lived outside the fold in a dangerous climate.

We waited impatiently for days when we could grasp some hope.

An email to friends on August 13, 2011, Sims' 38th birthday:

234

Dear friends,

I am sobbing with joy and a release of pain bottled up for way too long. I just had the most genuine conversation with Sims that I have had in several years. Today is his 38th birthday. The first miracle is he answered the phone. His pattern for over a year now is to not return phone calls, emails or texts from me. The second miracle is he was the "old Sims."

I am not foolish enough to think the "old Sims" has returned forever. And everyone receiving this email knows the "old Sims" presented a fair amount of challenges. But he was more open to me than he has been even on his best days. We talked about golf (he shot his best game ever yesterday) and about the possibility he could be a scratch golfer on the amateur circuit or make the UK team next year.

Another miracle, he said, "That's not why I'm playing golf. The studies have shown how much golf is therapeutic for PTSD." In the past he would not have admitted to me that he needed anything therapeutic and certainly would have been focused on making the amateur circuit or the UK team. So this is wonderful news.

I said at the end of the conversation, "Simmies, do you know I love you more than any person on the planet loves you? I know Tif and your children love you mightily, but I've loved you longer." He said, "I know, Mom, and I love you too." I don't have to tell any of you how much that means to me.

Thank you to each of you for the prayers, the listening ears, the concern and love you have given to me and to Sims. However temporary, today's call was a Balm in Gilead.

Happy happy birthday, Sims.

Love to each of you,

Bren

SCENE NINE

Resurrection & Redemption

We are the mirror as well as the face in it.
We are tasting the taste this minute of eternity.
We are pain and what cures pain.
We are the sweet cold water and the jar that pours.

— RUMI

John and I lulled away the hour in our peaceful church library enjoying the February scene out the big arched windows while grandson Tristan enjoyed KidsSing and Payden played in the nursery. This Wednesday evening routine, now well established, gave all four of us pleasure. My phone's text signal interrupted my reverie. A text from Sims: "Mom, when you drop Tristan off, would you please come in and chat for a minute."

On cue, my stomach tightened, pulse sped up, anxiety heightened — coming in to chat with Sims could mean anything from "I'm still furious with you for sending me to boarding school when I was nine years old" to "Would you babysit for the kids on Saturday" to "I love you and want you to know how grateful we are for all the support you give us with Tristan and Payden."

"Of course," I replied. "Yes, see you then."

As we entered the family room, Tiffany and Payden started playing and Tristan quickly joined them. The TV played in the background. Sims said, "Let's talk in here, Mom," as he guided me back to the living room. I sat down on the couch, but he perched on the arm near me. I felt his anxiety. It matched my own.

237

"Sure, what's up?"

"When we were driving home from Florida after Christmas, it came to me what I should do with my life. I need your help."

"I'm listening."

"I am starting an organization to give a voice and a face to child sexual abuse. I know you know how to start and work with non-profits and I would like for you to help us. We are going to climb The Seven Summits. Those are the highest mountains on each of the seven continents, Mom, in case you didn't know." He grins and gives me that look that melts women his age into puddles at his feet. "By climbing, publicizing and getting sponsors, we will raise money to fund education, advocacy and direct services to children or adult survivors of child sexual abuse. Then my main service will be to take survivors through healing wilderness adventures."

My mind raced. I've always taken in information quickly, especially as related to my children. So I gulped his statement down without chewing — mostly relieved the chat had turned out to be a positive subject.

Listen, don't talk.

But after a few details, he was ready for me to respond.

"Oh, Simmies, that is so extraordinary and you are perfect for the project! I'm so proud of you!"

Slow down. Be careful. What are you agreeing to?

I have two questions. First, are you sure you are ready to tell your story in public because you won't get away with not telling it? Second, are you sure it's me that you want to work with on this?"

I can't say no to this project anymore than I could stop being your mother. Oh my God, I'm so excited for you and so freakin' scared about working closely with you and what that could mean for our relationship. But I wouldn't say no to you in any lifetime.

"The answers, Mom, are 'yes' and 'yes.' I've given this two months of thought before asking you, and I'm ready to go."

I willed myself to look calm and supportive as my insides shook with swirls of emotion too complex to name individually. John and Tiffany had joined us in the living room by that time, but I didn't look at either of them. This moment was for Sims and me. No one else has traveled this journey with us. No one else fully understands. No one else will be walking across the tightrope of our relationship.

"Then, I'm ready to help you. I cannot take on actually doing the work, but I will serve as consultant to teach you and whoever how to do what needs to be done. Let's get started."

Neither John nor I slept that night. John's concern is for me. "You will get hurt again. Working together will make things worse instead of better."

I heard John's concerns, knew he was right and knew I could make no other choice but to say yes.

That evening, as on several other occasions in our lives, mine and Sims' relationship took a right angle turn. He began to talk, he shared ideas, emotions, plans, past hurts and even some anger. He started to return my phone calls, texts and initiated the same. The air in the house when we stopped by to pick up or drop off Tristan and Payden lightened appreciably. We began to share meals and, most important to Kentuckians, we shared the UK Wildcats' tenacious run to our eighth NCAA National Championship in March 2012. Great fun because there has never been anyone I enjoyed sharing UK basketball with more than my sons.

Sims and his small board of directors named the organization, Climb for Innocence. Starting a non-profit always presents a challenge for survival and funding, but as we have said with any task Sims has undertaken in life, "If he makes up his mind to do it, he will be successful." His grasp of the issues and a plethora of ideas on how to get funding have streamed from his mouth daily since that initial chat. Sponsors, news conferences, speaking engagements, key supporters, equipment needs, climbing schedule, legal documents. My delight at seeing him engaged, energized and excited makes saying yes seem reasonable.

As part of the founding documents of Climb for Innocence, Sims wrote his own brief bio. Reading his words for the first time brought tears of relief, guilt, gut-wrenching sorrow and pride that my son is continuing to fight for his life.

With any climb up the mountain, there will be twists and turn-backs. The founding of this non-profit ran headlong into its first obstacle with the sudden death of Sims' mentor and friend, Bazz Childress on April 5, 2012. Right after our shock and sorrow for Rachel and their daughters, John and I worried the effect Bazz's death would have on Sims and his recovery from PTSD and depression. In the midst of yet another loss would he be able to continue with his work? We feared for his well-being.

Bazz spent most of his time in what surely was the original man-cave, also known as his office. Sims and Bazz had been spending every Thursday together for the past year and a half. He and Sims spent hours discussing the plight of humanity — the profound and the puerile. After five heart attacks and a stroke, Bazz was on permanent disability. He may have been one of the most emotionally shutdown persons I have ever known. And Sims chose very few persons with whom to share his feelings. Somehow, these two men found solace in each other. War, death and near death as both had experienced them filled many hours of conversation.

Bazz had asked that Sims speak at his funeral if he were willing when the time came. This young man, who, since shooting himself three years earlier, had pulled himself into a hole and pulled the hole in after him, agreed he must speak at the service. Although Sims didn't have a lot of public speaking under his 38-year-old belt, he possessed natural skills and a deep, resonant voice inherited from his biological father, Dennis.

But he certainly had not been in public since this severe PTSD took over his life and persona. Would he be able to do it? He read the eulogy to John a few days before the funeral. He called me later and read it to me over the phone. The writing portion was done, and it was good.

One day that week when I stopped by his house, I dared to suggest, "Sims, Bazz's funeral will be people who already know you shot yourself and who have loved you for years. This would be a perfect setting for you to experience telling others how this near-death experience bonded you and Bazz. You have said you intend to tell that portion of your story in your non-profit work. Are you ready now?" And then I let the idea lie there and gestate.

As he walked to the pulpit in Central Baptist Church he looked like a GQ cover, his olive green suit stretched across his shoulders as crisp as any Marine uniform and he walked with pride. As he turned toward us, I saw his tight face, the color of dirty dish water.

Oh, please God, let him get through this. No standing ovation necessary, just stand tall and say your lines.

His first line was a joke that any one who knew Bazz would get, but would they laugh? After all, it was a funeral. They laughed and I saw the color return to his face. He was off and running. Bazz had taught Sims to read a compass and topographical map when Sims was a boy. Sims has used these tools in his work all over the world. He now used them as a metaphor for how Bazz gave him and so many others the tools to find their own direction in life and to make folks think for themselves. With ease, Sims made the point that after Bazz's heart attacks and his self-inflicted wound, they shared near death experiences in such a way that enabled them to help each other find peace.

I cried so hard, I was afraid some people thought I was Bazz's widow or his mother. I was just a mother witnessing the resurrection of her own son.

I wrote this letter to Sims shortly after his decision to found Climb for Innocence.

Dear Simmies,

Writing my memoir has been a healing process for me and I can't even begin to tell you how proud I am that you have started the journey of writing yours. My hope for you is that you will find as much balm for your wounds in the process as I have.

There will be points at which our memoirs intersect. I know I've told you a thousand times but I think I will need to say it over for the rest of my life — I am so sorry I sent you to a boarding school where you were molested by someone we both trusted.

We've been over the reasons we chose to send you to the school time and time again — how Dad and I had exhausted all resources available in Lexington. How coming from my poverty-ruled background, I believed that education was the key to most all of life's problems. To have a brilliant child stymied by severe dyslexia and ADHD and the monetary funds to address the issues — well, there would be no limit to the extent to which I would go to solve your problems.

If I could have known then, what I know now, I might have made any number of choices other than boarding school for a nine-year-old. We don't have the luxury of do-overs in life.

I'm here for you. I always have been and always will be.

Love,

Mom

I enjoy reclaiming religious words for the spiritual meaning that I think God originally intended — like the use of the word resurrection. I do not believe in the bodily resurrection of Jesus. I do, however, believe that resurrection from whatever grave has buried us is possible through God's love and the love of those around us. Sims has been resurrected to serve again by his own self-love, the love of his wife, children and, yes, his mother.

✂ ✂ ✂

A man who was careless about spiritual things died and went to hell. And he was much missed on earth by his old friends. His business manager went down to the gates of hell to see if there was a chance of bringing him back. But, though he pleaded for the gates to be opened, the iron bars never yielded. His cricket captain went also and besought Satan to let him out just for the remainder of the season. But there was no response. His minister went also and argued, saying, 'He wasn't altogether bad. Let him have another chance. Let him out just this once.' Many other friends of his went also and pleaded with Satan saying, Let him out. Let him out. Let him out.

But when his mother came she spoke no word of his release. Quietly, and with a strange catch in her voice, she said to Satan, 'Let me in.'

And immediately the great doors swung open upon their hinges. For love goes down through the gates of hell and there redeems the damned.

SOURCE UNKNOWN

The journey Sims and I have traveled as mother and son has led us both through hell and back. We have loved each other with a ferocity akin to mother tigers and cubs. We have fought and misunderstood each other in hurtful ways. While I want to stand on my high-horse and maintain that all I ever did was for his best interests, I know with the wisdom of age that I sometimes didn't understand his needs and wounds and desires. Our paths have been divergent; sometimes we couldn't even see across the trees where the other might be journeying. But I now know this: wherever life may lead either of us, at the end of any road, I'll be waiting there for him. No relationship has challenged me as much as ours, but as with most ventures that are difficult, having successfully accomplished the task, I can say all was worthwhile. I do not regret one second of time, one cent of money or one emotional investment that I have made in my first born, my first love.

As with the word resurrection, I believe the word redemption has far greater use than the narrow teaching of Christ redeeming us from our sins. I think we can experience redemption daily through the ups and downs of relationships. Sims and I continue to be redeemed through the hard work that we put in to loving each other and understanding each other.

Sims also provided several of the dearest relationships in my life: our now-deceased dog Spratley, our precious grandchildren, Tristan Robert (named after his uncle Mark Robert) and our granddaughter Payden Elise and our daughter-in-law Tiffany Corbin Bartella, who has proven her unconditional love for my son over and over again.

Spratley, Sims' dog purchased with a former girlfriend, was a chocolate Lab/border collie mix. Sims asked if John and I would keep her when he enlisted in the Marines in 2002. John and I fell in love with Sprats before we knew how much her coat shedded, but she provided immense pleasure in addition to dust bunnies. Sims trained her to work in a wilderness program with him so she was highly disciplined. This son, who never met a rule he thought applied to him, instilled in this canine a devotion to authority that Sims gave only to the military. Spratley died of spleen tumors while I was writing this memoir. When asked why he didn't take Spratley back after leaving the military, Sims answered, "Because she saved my mother's life." Yes, Spratley was there to push up against me, make me laugh and make me walk when I trudged through the trenches of grief over Mark's death. Even science has caught up with what dog lovers have known for centuries: a good dog can save a life.

With the pace of a glacier Sims and I are healing our relationship. We tread gingerly around each other's soft spots. We govern, delete and couch our responses. The sense of humor we share that has lain buried beneath too many winters of misunderstandings peeks out with the hope of spring's first jonquil.

Act Four

SCENE ONE

The Joy of a Fourth Act

The Promised Land always lies
on the other side of a Wilderness.

— HAVELOCK ELLIS

Joy, rather than happiness, is the goal of life,
for joy is the emotion which accompanies
our fulfilling our natures as human beings.

— ROLLO MAY

When John and I returned to Lexington in 2011, I had not fully grasped the joy that lay before me. Yes, I had heard other grandparents, covered in the stickiness of Skittles and chocolate milk, spewing forth praise of grandchildren. But you don't know what you don't know. I thought I had loved my children with all the intensity I was capable of. And I had and still do. I now understand what other grandmothers have tried to tell me. There is a quality of peace, renewal and deliciousness in loving grandchildren that is unlike all other loves. At three years of age, grandson Tristan ran in to my arms and said, "Mimi, when I was a little boy I fell in love with you." I have been Play-Doh in his hands ever since.

Perhaps because all other roles have played out on the stage. Perhaps because wisdom convinced me I deserve this role. Perhaps because I have finally learned through tragedy and turmoil to be in the present. Regardless of reason, I don the costume of Mimi and revel in making my entrance in this fourth act of pure joy.

Tristan has spent most Saturday nights with us since our return to Lexington. Then five, his tiny hands twisted, turned, jittered and pulsed as he tried to soothe his hyperactive body into sleep. For reasons I don't understand, twisting and turning one hand under my torso became part of the sleepy-dance on the nights he spent with Pappa and me. Mimi, who also has rituals for getting her body to sleep, learned to accept the wiggly little hands.

He requested that bedtime reading consist of two parts Mimi reading and one part Tristan reading aloud. His personal favorite, Garfield cartoon books, came with bittersweet memories since the collection belonged to his Uncle Mark, whom Tristan never knew except through pictures and stories.

We giggled at Garfield and Odie. If we didn't get the joke, we called the cartoon dumb and moved on. Sometimes Mimi explained an adult concept but explaining usually ruined the spontaneity and the joke.

When sleep came for him, I laid there beside his long, wiry body, amazed that once again I have been given the gift of loving and relating to this miracle of life. Being close to this next generation of my own DNA is an extra inning, a fourth act in the drama, a miracle cure for all of life's wounds.

One Sunday as we were driving to church and Pappa was grumpy about something. Tristan's child-like voice exuded adulthood when, from the back seat, he said, "Pappa! Really! Do you want to act like that right now?" We laughed so hard it totally ended Pappa's grumpiness.

After church I asked Tristan what the Worship and Wonder story was for that day. "Noah's Ark," he said, "I know everything about Noah's ark now. I even know that those two pigeons flew up and made their freakin' nest on the top of the ark."

I practically gasped and said, "Tristan, we don't use freakin' at church."

"But it's not a bad word, Mimi," he said.

"No, but it's not a church word."

He pulled me down to his level as we walked and whispered, "But we can use it at your house, right, Mimi?"

I'm forced to ponder anew where I stand on raucous, naughty, semi-bad or down-right gross language with these new children in my life.

When we discovered only half of our Christmas tree made the move from Raleigh to Lexington, Tristan and I set out to buy a new one on a rainy, cold Sunday afternoon. What was I thinking? Michael's, the arts and craft store, was crowded and a little boy's wonderland of distraction.

When we finally accomplished our goal and a dear-to-my-heart employee helped us get the tree into the car, I turned to Tristan and said, "We did it! Tristan and Mimi bought the new Christmas tree and we got a *big ass* tree!"

Appalled, Tristan shouted, "Off to Bad Languageville. Population: YOU!"

When my children were pre-teens, I explained to them, "Language is neither moral nor immoral. But it is appropriate and inappropriate to particular situations." Of course, they had to push the limits of my explanation, most significantly by dropping the f-bomb to their Great-Aunt BJ, the retired missionary. So much for that parenting technique. Maybe I'll do better with my grandchildren.

Being an overachiever from birth, I wanted to ace this grandparenting gig. We finally declared we were ready for our first sleepover with *both* precious angels. Tristan was five at that time and Payden was 12 months.

Let me clarify. I started decorating our guest room for these little creatures before we left North Carolina, neutral to accommodate both boy and girl. Cute but not so cutesy we couldn't use it for an adult guest room when necessary. Lots of toys, books, pictures, just what I wanted it to be. Only one problem: My perfect angels are too scared to sleep in there.

We have a king-size Tempur-Pedic bed, but I also have a king-size husband. John is 6'5" and as Tristan likes to tell everyone, "My Pappa used to be a Viking." (Please do not tell Tristan that just means he's Scandinavian and Minnesotan and has very big shoulders.) The strategy was to get Tristan to sleep in our bed then put him on a pallet on the floor and let the little princess sleep with us. My daughter-in-law assured me this plan would work because Tristan could be moved without waking up and would not realize he'd been moved until morning.

Our plan worked like a well-oiled Swiss machine for the first half of the night. I had already been having a restless sleep because I was concerned the Viking would roll over on the Princess. I finally experienced true rest with my back toward both of them leaving the Princess in God's hands. Then I awakened to gentle pushing against my back. *Payden sure is pushing hard against me for such a little thing.* I rolled over intending to center her in the bed so I could get back to sleep. As I looked at the little tow-head beside me, I had to blink my sleepy eyes several times before accepting it was Tristan. He awakened during the night, thought he had fallen out of bed and crawled back in. We were now four-in-a-bed.

There was no Plan B so we all cuddled up and got whatever sleep would come. Since deep sleep came slowly, Tristan, Payden and I all slept too late to get the four of us fed and dressed for church. At that point, I was feeling grandparent failure creeping up on me like Ghostbuster slime. I wanted the two beautifully dressed and coiffed grandchildren in church with me that day. Oh well, maybe next time. I was amazed by the ease with which I let go of the Rockwell image and leaned into the moment.

Pappa fixed his world-famous waffles for breakfast, and we gobbled them down with fruit and milk. He rushed off to church without us. The yummy-ness of having both angels with me surpassed any waffle, famous or not. Tristan was entertaining himself in the family room and Payden was getting a big dose of Mimi-love. I decided that I could at least put the refrigerated items away from the breakfast table. So with Payden on my hip, I picked up the little brown jug of maple syrup to move it to the fridge. As I turned away from the table, I lost my grip on the syrup. It not only spilled, it bounced, as syrup poured over the floor and spattered up the walls of the breakfast room.

At that instant, a "tweet" went out to the entire world of black ants, "Syrup feast at the Peterson household. One hundred percent maple syrup. No preservatives, no corn syrup. Come one, come all."

And they did. *Instantly.*

I was impressed with myself that I got Tristan to play with Payden long enough to mop the kitchen and breakfast room with the hottest, soapiest water I could make. I was not so impressed that even that process did not get all the stickiness up, so Payden crawled around with the ants until I got her in the tub.

Surely, next time will be easier. But I filed the story away to tell and retell to Tristan and Payden in the coming years.

In three lightning fast years, Payden Elise has grown from chunky baby with almost no hair into a miniature blond three-year-old diva who actually loves getting shoes, clothes and bling for her birthday. I am astounded at my good fortune in being able to grandparent her. Bows, jewelry, glitter, cowgirl boots and Disney figures clutter our home as soon as she arrives. She seems to have inherited more than a modicum of her Mimi's sass and bossiness, a full portion of her Daddy's fortitude and her Mommy's delicate nose.

On Payden's first visit to Explorium, the Lexington children's museum, she glowed with the excitement of being out with big brother and soaked the sensory experiences up as if new worlds had opened. Tristan soon became occupied on his own. Payden, not quite two then, surveyed the room, accepted that Tristan was busy then turned her tiny face up to Pappa and me demanding, "Follow me!" No doubt an omen of the future with this girl.

Her exploding vocabulary brings new sentences with each visit. Most recently, it was, "Don't worry, Mimi, I got this." Didn't matter what the subject was, she was in charge.

The role of Mimi clarifies for me with each passing scene. With bemusement, I ponder my previous roles — nerd, missionary, glamour girl, mother, widow, grief expert — wisdom chiseled out one chip at a time. Like any older actor, only I know the extent to which my previous roles inform the current one. But with a few rehearsals under my belt, I grasp the essence of this Mimi gig. I am Appreciator-in-Chief, with the good fortune of grandchildren who are writing a new script.

❧ ❧ ❧

Tristan's script provides laughter and gives us pause at the wisdom of children.

Pappa had a photography exhibit opening soon. Tristan came over before all the photos were to be delivered to the Woodford County Library. I gave him one of the publicity cards and invited him to see a few of the photos that were in tubs in the living room. I encouraged him to take the card home to Mommy and Daddy to remind them to bring him to the exhibit. He looked with interest at the photos we unwrapped and went on with his playing. In a few minutes, he declared, "Mimi, I'm not the kind of boy who goes somewhere just to look at pictures."

From birth, Tristan adopted the attitude that he could win at anything and everything and perhaps it is even his Divine Right to win every game. He and I were racing cars while he soaked in the tub at about age four. I allowed him to win the first two races and then made sure I won the third. I whooped and hollered in victory. He gently touched my arm and chided, "Mimi, let's play nice and be friends."

On Easter morning 2011, Tristan awakened in our bed and I asked, "Do you want to get up now and go wish Pappa a Happy Easter?"

"No," he answered, "let's just lie here and enjoy this Easter moment."

I didn't know five-year-olds had Easter moments.

One morning, Tristan and I had a conversation about tears because he saw me putting eye drops in and asked what they were. I explained the medical necessity and went on to joke about them being tears of joy because he was spending the night. I asked if he had ever cried tears of joy because something was so wonderful, joyful or emotional. He didn't have to blink an eye before responding, "Yes, in the movie *Mee-Shee* because the music was so beautiful!" He was speaking of Jim Henson's movie, *Mee-Shee: The Water Giant*. I have no idea how long ago he saw that movie but not recently. Music moves his soul, and he remembers even small details about the pieces he hears.

Tristan knows his Uncle Mark — never mind that Uncle Mark died three years before he was born. For example, we were at Applebee's one evening when Tristan ordered French fries and an order of bacon. I ordered potato skins which, of course, had bacon on them. I said, "Tristan, look we're having the same thing, potatoes and bacon. What else do we both like?"

Without missing a bite, he answered, "We both love Uncle Mark."

Yes, Art Linkletter, kids still say the darndest things.

Another Sunday morning, Tristan said, "Mimi, you and Pappa use different words than my Mommy and Daddy." We took that as a cue that he loved vocabulary words so we began the tradition of learning a new word each Sunday to share with our friend Don Lichtenfelt at church. Then one Sunday as this tradition was taking place, another friend, remarked, "Oh, Tristan, you are a sesquipedalian. I am, too!" So Tristan will tell you he is a sesquipedalian and what that means. But when I asked if he had told his new first-grade teacher about his love of words, he replied, "Mimi, she's not like you. She doesn't care about all those words." I hope he got that wrong, and I suspected that he didn't want to draw undue attention to himself.

I have pondered whether Tristan will be the next Dale Earnhardt, Jr. on the NASCAR circuit, the curator of the Smithsonian or conductor of our local philharmonic. His play time last year hinted of all three careers.

As NASCAR driver he required the services of the "manager" — another role for his Mimi. He preferred I "manage" — really the job of announcing — because I captured his imagination about how race day excitement and events unfolded.

"Ladies and Gentlemen, welcome to NASCAR. You are in for the most exciting day in racing and you will not be disappointed!" His preference for Mimi had nothing to about drama and the glib tongue.

Based on the engaging *Cars* movie, Tristan's cast metal and plastic cars all possessed personalities and moral characteristics. We lined them up, made a place for the pit crew and for President Barack Obama's limousine and entourage. Tristan always got to be Lightning McQueen who won every race. He divided the cars into various countries; I could always expect Japanese, Chinese, British and Italian cars. So the Manager had to develop, at minimum, British, Italian and Asian accents.

One day, Francesco, the bad guy, broke a NASCAR rule, and the Manager called for an investigation, penalty and fine. I must have been on a roll as Francesco's angry mother who attended the race. I ranted and raved in my best Italian accent. So well, in fact, that Tristan broke character and inquired, "Mi — — — —-mi, are you mad at me or are you still being Francesco's mommy?" I played my part well. My little NASCAR fan also confused whether the driver breaking the rules had to be accountable to the track rules or his mommy. Guess we know where his locus of authority still rests.

In addition to NASCAR driver, Tristan created a museum and played the role of museum director with an all-knowing voice, a proper carriage with hands behind his back and an officious gait to assure you knew who was in charge. "Our museum houses the traditional dinosaurs and historical exhibits as well as some new exhibits I have created." Using toys as props, the tour displayed the length and width and breadth of his knowledge and took hours and several rooms of the house to create.

Pappa and I were most impressed with one of those "new" exhibits, a memorial he built to dead soldiers. Remember this six-year-old museum director's daddy was a Marine who lost friends in Iraq and Afghanistan. A cardboard box rested on the floor with a child's plastic chair on it, atop the box was a riderless motorcycle. The museum director, in his compassionate but professional voice, informed us, "This box contains the belongings and memories of a soldier who was killed in war." Then he artfully, let that comment rest in silence.

Still in the mood for museum directing when we had to leave his house, Tristan pretended the entire city comprised his museum as we drove to our destination. From the back seat, we heard his imitation of a grown-up voice describing every building, fireplug and tree. We played along and asked questions of "The Director." He hesitated but a moment, then with an officious, "We — — — — ll, that fire plug is painted yellow and green instead of red because schoolchildren wanted to paint it that way." He never lacked an answer regardless of the question. All the world was Tristan's museum.

Tristan's third career last year was music conductor. Pappa and I took him to the children's concert of the Lexington Philharmonic. We sat in a box partially overlooking the stage and the pit. He asked, "Are those black curtains going to open up and people will come out in costumes?"

257

"No, Tristan, this is a concert not a play or musical," Mimi replied.

"Okay, then I'm not going to like it. I will be bored."

"Let's listen to the few pieces that will be played before the drum ensemble which is what we thought you would like. Then if after the drums you want to go home, we will go home."

"It's a deal, Mimi."

We were only one piece into the drum program when he proclaimed, "I like this!" We stayed to the end. Unfortunately, Tristan carried his conducting debut too far by directing his church choir teacher instead of singing. His teacher squatted down to his level and gently told him, "Tristan, there is only one director of this choir and it's me. Understand?"

Those beautiful blue eyes looked sheepish as he said, "Sometimes I go overboard."

As Tristan continues to write his own script and Payden explores her world, Mimi relishes her role as appreciator and sees life through new eyes.

On vacation, Tristan and Mommy went to the hot dog stand at the beach. When Mommy handed him his hot dog, he marched right over and sat at the only table nearby. There were two elderly people, dressed in turtlenecks and sweaters, and a woman in her 50s who appeared to be their daughter.

Mommy inquired, "Is it okay if he sits there to eat his hot dog?"

Thinking he was this darling sweet child, they quickly agreed.

Being acquainted with "retiring to Florida," Tristan asked, "Did you move down here to retire?"

"Why, yes, we did," replied the old man.

"Better be careful," Tristan responds, "You retire, move to Florida and BOOM (as he claps his hands), graveyard!"

The old folks quickly finished their lunch and moved on.

Tristan seems well acquainted with this dying business. From the back seat of our car one day, he informed me, "Mimi, you *will* die some day. It's the cycle of life you know."

Until then, I'm grateful every day for spending my fourth act with Tristan and Payden Bartella.

CLOSING

Portraiture Faces

The very angels themselves cannot persuade
the wretched and blundering children on earth
as can one human being broken on the wheels of living.
In Love's service, only the wounded soldiers can serve.

— THORTON WILDER,
from *An Angel That Troubled the Waters*

"I can't — supper, sick — I can't — no, I mean — I fix — I'm not — no, too supper, no, too sick."

I tried hard to construct two sentences that would communicate that I was too sick to prepare supper. That attempted utterance would be the last I remembered for four days. John would tell me later that when he realized his sassy, motor-mouth wife could not speak, he knew it was time to head to the emergency room.

"The light," he recalled, "at the intersection of Rosemont Garden and Nicholasville Road seemed like an eternity as I watched you slumped over in the front seat. I talked to you encouraging you to "hang in there," "don't give up, Bren, breathe" and "we're almost there.""

He remembered feeling that the emergency room personnel moved in slow motion. He wanted action. Answers. I stunned him by sitting up, answering questions, producing my health care cards and identification. I have no memory of that. Finally, the doctor ruled out stroke and heart attack. By that time, my son Sims was there, and he and John held me still as the ER doctor performed the spinal tap and pronounced the diagnosis: bacterial meningitis.

Meningitis is the infection and inflammation of the meninges that are the three membranes covering the brain and spinal cord. The ER doctor also told John at that time that if he had brought me to the hospital even hours later, I would be dead. Meningitis is curable but scary. Scary because death can come so quickly, and, if one lives the possibilities of residual damage are numerous: compromised vision, damaged or no hearing, loss of motor skills including ability to walk and, of course, memory and brain function. However, several doctors reminded me I was closest to the scenario of death.

"Really? Did I need another reminder of how fragile and precious life is?"
— Brenda, upon coming out of the fog.

I knew Central Baptist Hospital very well. I had logged hundreds of hours there in the past — with Dennis, with Bart's multiple surgeries, one surgery of my own, pastoral care visits and personal visits to friends and family. But I have no visual image of those hours in March 2013 or of that emergency room. My intellect knows what I should have seen and felt, but I have no memory of the doctor's face, the physical layout of the room, the pain of needle sticks, the feel of a gurney, the action of someone removing my clothes. Nothing, except an oval view of significant faces and the sound of voices that were familiar and dear to me. The background seemed black, non-existent, but faces seemed to hang in oval portraiture frames around me. Michael Rintimaa, our dear friend, characteristically quiet, stood close by John sharing his concern and love. Sims, reserved and withdrawn, watched every move made toward me. I could feel that he was nervous. I saw their faces, I felt their love. But I saw no faces of the hospital personnel.

After the diagnosis, I was moved into the Intensive Care Unit. Friday night, Saturday, Sunday and Monday, I again have no memory of my physical surroundings, and, yet, the faces of those who visited those days came through to my swollen brain like headlights on a dark road ahead. Rachel's laugh rang through to me when she cackled because I demanded a microwave in ICU when I wanted a baked potato. I saw Mary standing by my side smiling but silently saying a prayer. I felt an extra dose of comfort when Rhonda visited because I knew her vast medical knowledge would question everything. One day, John awakened me and asked, "Do you know these folks." I sat upright in my bed, pronounced them to be Betty and Jim Cecil and went back to sleep. I don't remember another word spoken, but I remember their faces at the foot of my bed.

Sims visited every evening, and I grasped at his hands and drank in every feature of his face as if my memory might fail me even on the most precious of people. John was a daily visitor, and his touch and his voice healed as much as any drug. Rosemary walked in the door one day delivering an inside joke that only she and I remember. Anne brought me trash reading because my brain was supposed to rest. Wendy's laughter could cure an entire hospital of patients.

Faces. Faces of people I love and people who love me.

As the week wore on I became more cognizant of surroundings. I moved out of ICU into a regular room, and I can remember the environment of that room. Tiffany brought Tristan and Payden to visit one day, creating the best memory of the challenging experience. The hospital staff provided an ice cream party on my bed and the children decided the control panel on my bed was Mission Control at NASA so they launched rockets and moved Mimi up and down at will.

After seven days, I went home but still had to go back to the hospital every day for antibiotic infusions. The doctors assured me that I was alive because of timing: the miracle of when John took me to the ER — yes, the doctors used the word "miracle." They also marveled at me having an immune system that hit a home run. During my grief over Mark's death and when Sims shot himself, my immune system was compromised and could not have stepped up if needed. Modestly, when pushed, my doctors admitted that I had a stellar medical team also. It appeared that I would have zero residual damage. Fatigue, yes. Profound fatigue. Headaches when I'm tired still remind me to take it easy. And the docs also cautioned that it would take one full year for my body to completely recover.

I went home with yet another reminder of values, priorities, who I am, why I'm here. There's nothing quite like being hours from death to reiterate what you've learned in a lifetime. Faces. Faces of people who have and will stand in the gap for me. Whatever the gaps have been in my life, there have been people who have bridged those divides so that I could cross over to the other side. Relationships form the web that supports all life.

Being born into poverty and pandemonium demanded that I figure out my own place in this world. But the task belongs to each of us. The work takes greater effort when we are born into tumult and dysfunction. I wandered aimlessly at times in finding my place but came to rest comfortably in the knowledge of who I am.

Humanity is not on a ladder with some people lower and others higher, rather we are all part of a circle. We need not fear or envy those we perceive to have more wealth, higher positions or more education. We need not pity those who have less. If more folks join the circle we make the circle bigger so we can all see each other's faces and hear each other's stories. The trappings of wealth, position and education cannot put people back on the ladder. Let's reject that premise for life.

Though I have experienced more than my share of obstacles in life, I have also been blessed. And as long as I hold on to hope, even those times when I felt like I was holding a piece of wet spaghetti, I can still proclaim there is more for me to contribute in this lifetime.

Resources

Books That Have Formed Me

Bragg, Rick, *All Over But The Shoutin'*, Pantheon Books, 1997.

Brown, Brene, *The Gifts of Imperfection*, Hazelden, 2010.

———, *I Thought It Was Just Me (but it isn't)*, Gotham Books, 2007.

Cousins, Norman, *Anatomy of an Illness*, W.W. Norton, 1979.

———, *Head First*, E. P. Dutton, 1989.

Didion, Joan, *The Year of Magical Thinking*, Alfred A. Knopf, 2005.

Frankl, Viktor, *Man's Search for Meaning*, Beacon, 1959.

Fuller, Robert W., *Somebodies and Nobodies: Overcoming the Abuse of Rank*, New Society Publishers, 2004, 209 pages.

Fulghum, Robert, *All I Ever Need to Know I Learned in Kindergarten*, Villard Books, 1988.

Gilbert, Elizabeth, *Eat, Pray, Love: One Woman's Search for Everything Across Italy, India and Indonesia*, Penguin Books, 2006.

Irving, John, *Prayer for Owen Meany*, William Morrow, 1989.

Jeffers, Susan, *Feel the Fear And Do It Anyway*, Ballantine Books, 1987.

Kidd, Sue Monk, *The Secret Life of Bees*, Penguin, 2003.

———, *When the Heart Waits: Spiritual Direction for Life's Sacred Questions*, HarperSan Francisco, 1990.

Kingsolver, Barbara, *The Poisonwood Bible*, HarperCollins, 1998.

LaMott, Anne, *Bird by Bird: Some Instructions on Writing and Life*, Anchor Books, 1994.

———, *Grace (Eventually): Some Thoughts on Faith*, Riverhead, 2007.

———, *Traveling Mercies: Some Thoughts on Faith*. Anchor, 2001.

———, *Plan B: Further Thoughts on Faith*. Riverhead, 2005.

McGoldrick, Monica; and Gerson, Randy and Petry, Suel, *Genograms: Assessment and Intervention*, 1985, Third Ed., W.W. Norton, 2008

Muller, Wayne, *Legacy of the Heart*. Fireside, 1992.

Oates, Wayne. *The Struggle to be Free: My Story and Your Story*, Westminster / John Knox Press, 1983.

Peck, Scott, T*he Road Less Traveled,* Simon and Schuster, 1978.

Pink, Daniel, *A Whole New Mind: Why Right-Brainers Will Rule the Future*, Berkley Publishing, 2005.

Reed, John P., *When You Feel Insecure*, Westminster / John Knox Press, 1989.

Stockett, Kathryn, *The Help*, Amy Einhorn, 2009.

Tannen, Deborah, *You Were Always Mom's Favorite! Sisters in Conversation Throughout Their Lives,* Ballantine, 2009.

Taylor, Barbara Brown, *An Altar in the World: A Geography of Faith. HarperCollins, 2009.*

Viorst, Judith, *Necessary Losses. Fireside, 1986.*

————, *Suddenly Sixty and Other Shocks of Later Life,* Simon & Schuster, 2000.

————, *Too Young To Be Seventy,* Free Press, 2005.

————, *Grown Up Marriage: What we know, wish we had known and still need to know about being married,* Free Press, 2003.

Discussion Guide for Reading Groups

- How does the position/status you were born into affect your life today?

- How did the author come to define "home?"

- Can you see any advantages to constantly moving as a child versus the stability of growing up in the same place?

- What family relationships defined the author's life? Who was her most positive role model? What family relationships form your adult life?

- The author had many tragic events in her life. If you had experienced these events would you have questioned God or lost your faith? Why do you think she didn't?

- When the author was asked not to help her family financially, she honored that promise by not helping her mother and not taking in one sibling and broke it by helping another sibling. Discuss when she was right and when she was wrong.

- The author maintains that education, community and spirituality are means by which we can know ourselves and give to others. Which path do you use? Give specific examples.

- Who in your life holds up the mirror to help you discover who you are?

Another Form of Resurrection: Organ Donation

LETTER FROM HEART RECIPIENT

My name is Jerry. I am the recipient of your loved one's heart.

I have been married for 30 plus years to a wonderful woman. We have two sons. The eldest son is married. They have 3 girls and one boy. The other son is single. I am confident I would not have been able to see my only grandson without the donation of your loved one's heart.

Your son's gift has provided me with a new start on life. I can now resume the activities I love which were fishing and woodworking. My wife and I have been able to enjoy the beginning of our retirement years. She taught in public schools for twenty-five years. The first trip we took after being released by the hospital was to visit our grandchildren.

I have been blessed by your loved one's gift. As a matter of note, my sons have signed-up for the organ donors program.

I have no idea if you are of the Christian faith however, I have asked God to bless you and your family as your loved one's heart donation has been a blessing to me and my family.

Love to you all

In addition to Mark's heart donation, his liver was transplanted into a 41 year old man from San Antonio. His right kidney went to a 39 year old man with a wife and two children who lost his own kidney to multiple infections. The left kidney went to a 52 year old woman who has worked in childcare all of her life.

Mark's bones were sent to the Musculotskeletal Transplant Foundation to be used to reconstruct bone of those suffering from crippling disease or injury, which may have resulted in the prevention of amputations, the restoration of movement, or countless other benefits.

His skin was sent to Shriner's Burn Center for Children and was used to aid in the recovery of those who have been severely burned.

His veins were recovered by LifeGift Organ Donation Center for CryoLife and were used in patients requiring arterial bypass surgery.

His beautiful blue eyes were used for their corneas which were sent to Lions Eye Bank and were used to improve or restore sight to those with eye disease or injury.

The dura matter of his extraordinary brain was sent to Transplant Research Foundation and was used to replace dura in patients having brain surgery.

There is resurrection all around us. I encourage you to consider organ donation if you are in a position to make this life-giving decision. I chuckle thinking these folks who received parts of my Mark might become uncontrollably funny one day. Mark lives.

List of Illustrations

Author's Note & Acknowledgments

A memoir is a constructed view of reality.

— TAMIM ANSARY,
author of *West of Kabul, East of New York*

This book is my attempt to be understood — my reality, no one else's. My truth. While those who have joined me on this journey may disagree with me about facts, there can be no disagreement that my story is my truth, as I alone experienced life.

W.E.B. DeBois stated, "Autobiographies do not form indisputable authorities. They are always incomplete, and often unreliable. Eager as I am to put down my truth, there are difficulties; memory fails especially in small details, so that it becomes finally but a theory of my life, with much forgotten and misconceived, with valuable testimony but often less than absolutely true, despite my intention to be frank and fair."

I have attempted to be "frank and fair" within the context of my own experience, even to the point of remembering actual dialogue. What you have here is my Truth, and much of it is fact. Many names have been changed to protect the guilty and the innocent.

The long and sometimes difficult task of writing a memoir includes reliving your life — not always willingly. I could not have completed the task without the "girlfriends who get you through life." Thank you to Leah Bartella, Linda Carruth Davis, Rhonda Johnston, Lisa Johnston, Martha Johnston Dryden, Mary Henson, Rosemary Wimpling, Wendy Wilson, Lynn "Boog" Bova, Rachel Smith Childress, Vonda Lichtenfelt, Bookie Wilson, Margaret Mills and Laura Sullivan.

There is so much more to a finished book that the writing of the words. I'm grateful for the skill and talent of Rita Gatton, copy writer extraordinaire, Jonathan Greene for interior design and the inimitable and uber-talented Carol Nix for cover design.

The Carnegie Center for Literacy in Lexington, KY nurtured me as a writer and provided a community of writing friends who hold you up and cheer you on. But this book would not be in your hands now if not for the guidance, encouragement and wisdom of Leatha Kendrick, my friend, editor and guru. Thank you, dear Leatha. Don Lichtenfelt has also played a significant role in the completion of this book. Conversations with Don, too many to count, have formed words, phrases and complete stories of this finished memoir. Thank and You seem like small words when spoken in gratitude for large acts of friendship.

My heart bursts with love and gratitude for my son, Sims Bartella and his precious family of Tiffany, Tristan and Payden. Wherever you roam, dear Sims, I will be beside you, in front of you and waiting at the end of the road.

Finally, my partner in all of life, John Lynner Peterson, my heart belongs to you.

About the Author

Brenda Bartella Peterson's speaking mantra is "keep it real." Her topics, her life stories and her humor all point toward the goal of teaching others to live authentically.

Brenda's career path reflects multiple skills and interests. She was the senior advisor for Religious Outreach for the Democratic National Committee and executive director of Clergy Leadership Network, the first religious-left political action committee.

Brenda has been a corporate trainer, non-profit executive and minister as well as successful speaker and writer. Her writing can be viewed on her website and blog at www.brendabartellapeterson.com and on www.norehearsal.net

Brenda and her husband, John, live in Lexington, Kentucky to be near the brightest, prettiest, most charming grandchildren the world has ever known, objectively speaking, of course.

Brenda's husband, John Lynner Peterson, is a photographer whose work can be seen at www.johnlynnerpeterson.com.

This book has been typeset in Agmena Pro
designed by Jovica Veljovic in 2012.
Design by Jonathan Greene.
Printing & binding by
BookMobile.